Dolls' Clothes

Mette Jørgensen

Illustrated by Jette R. Ternsøe

DAVID PORTEOUS

CHUDLEIGH • DEVON

Contents

Introduction 5

Before you begin 6

Underwear 7
- Vest and underpants
- Knickers
- Petticoat

Nightclothes 10
- Nightdress
- Dressing gown

T-shirts and blouses 13
- T-shirt with set-in sleeves
- Short-sleeved T-shirt
- Blouse with puffed sleeves

Trousers 17
- Culottes
- Pleated trousers
- Baby trousers
- Dungarees
- Trousers with bib
- Shorts

Skirts 26
- Skirt
- Skirt with bib
- Skirt with straps

Bikini top 30

Dresses 32
- Dress with puffed sleeves
- Dress with pin tucks

Jackets and tops 36
- Jacket
- Braid-trimmed jacket
- Jogging clothes
- Track suit
- Blouson jacket and skirt

Romper suit 42

Outdoor clothes 44
- Jacket
- Coat
- Ski wear
- Rainwear

Fancy dress 49
- Pierrot costume

Knitwear 50
- Patterned sweater
- Cardigan

Accessories 52
- Sun hat
- Lace collar
- Hat and scarf
- Shoulder bag
- Tote bag

Helpful hints 56

Templates 62

Index 93

Introduction

Making your own dolls' clothes is fun, as well as being an inexpensive and creative hobby. It is also a good way to get to know your sewing machine, if you do not have much experience of working with it.

This book includes patterns and instructions for sewing a complete wardrobe for dolls from 38cm (15in) to 58cm (23in) tall. The patterns range from the simple to the more difficult, and there are suggestions on ways to vary the basic patterns. Every effort has been made to make each pattern as easy to stitch as possible, and zips, buttons and buttonholes are not used. The clothes can be made prettier or smarter depending on your choice of materials and colours.

Remnants of material are ideal for sewing dolls' clothes, but it is not an expensive hobby even if you decide to buy special material. It is a good idea to look in curtain shops and craft shops, which often have off-cuts of beautiful and unusual fabrics. Otherwise, you can use any kind of remnants to work with – discarded tablecloths and bed linen, as well as curtains, clothes and so on.

With only very little effort, the finished dolls' clothes can be made to look really exciting and "professional". Look in fabric and craft shops for fancy borders, trimmings, short lengths of lace, iron-on decorations and so on.

The most exciting thing is to create something yourself, so use the patterns and the methods shown in the book as a starting point, and go on from there.

I hope the book will give you ideas for many hours of creative work, for the enjoyment both of those doing the sewing and of those whose dolls receive their very own wardrobe.

Before you begin

All the patterns are given in three sizes. Before you begin to stitch, measure the height of the doll and find the appropriate pattern:
Small: 38–45cm (15–17³/₄in)
Medium: 46–52cm (18–20¹/₂in)
Large: 53–58cm (21–23in)

All the patterns include a seam allowance, so you do not need to add this when you are cutting out the material. Unless otherwise indicated, the seam allowance throughout is 1cm (¹/₂in).

The patterns are graded according to their level of difficulty:

Easy

A little more difficult

A little more demanding or has complicated details

The instructions for each pattern explain the order in which you should stitch, and there are photographs and drawings of all the patterns, as well as suggestions on choosing materials. You will find it easier to stitch if you press open the seams and iron edges flat as you work.

Techniques that are used in more than one design are marked with an asterisk (*), and these are described in more detail on pages 56–61.

There are many different sizes of doll, each with its individual measurements. The patterns in the book are generously sized, but before you cut out any material, check that your doll's waist, arm and leg will fit the measurements in the pattern. If there are large discrepancies, adjust the pattern slightly or choose a larger size. Leg and sleeve lengths can simply be made longer or shorter according to the size of the doll. The waist size is important, but patterns that have elasticated waists can easily be adapted to quite large differences by making the elastic longer or shorter. Patterns with non-stretch waistbands can be made wider or smaller by varying the number or depth of the tucks. Remember to increase or shorten the length of the waistband to suit the measurement of the doll.

Vest and underpants 🧸

The pattern for this set of underclothes is best suited to dolls that do not have fabric bodies. Use a stretchy material, like jersey, and work with 6mm ($^1/_4$in) seam allowances. The edges do not need to be zigzagged as the seams are sewn with lockstitch or with a small zigzag stitch.

Underpants

Using the template on page 62, place the pattern along the fold and cut out one piece.

Fold over the leg openings by 6mm ($^1/_4$in) and stitch the seams

Stitch the side seams together.

Make a casing* at the waist and pull through the elastic.

Vest

Use the templates on page 62 to cut out one front and one back.

Stitch the shoulder seams.

Fold over the neck opening by 6mm ($^1/_4$in) and stitch.

Fold over the sleeve openings by 6mm ($^1/_4$in) and stitch.

Stitch the side seams together.

Turn up the hem of the vest.

Note You could put a short length of lace at the front of the neckline or attach a little artificial rose.

Knickers

The knickers should be made with a thin, white, cotton material, such as broderie anglaise. They have a casing to hold elastic at the waist, and sewn-in elastic in the legs. The legs are edged with lace. Work with a seam allowance of 1cm ($\frac{1}{2}$in), unless otherwise indicated. There are patterns for knickers with both long and short legs. A pretty effect can be obtained by sewing the knickers in material that matches the colour of the rest of the doll's clothing – for example, rose-coloured pantaloons with a pink skirt.

Use the templates on page 64 to cut two fronts and two backs.

Measure a piece of elastic round the doll's legs, making sure it is not too tight. Stitch the elastic on the reverse side of the legs with small zigzag stitches, about 2cm ($\frac{3}{4}$in) from the edge and beginning and ending about 1cm ($\frac{1}{2}$in) in from the edge of the material (to allow for the seams). Stretch the elastic while you stitch to fit the width of the leg.

Stitch the side seams.

Fold down the waist by 2cm ($\frac{3}{4}$in) and make a casing*. Measure a length of elastic according to the doll's waist and pull it through the casing.

Short legs

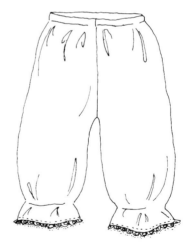

Pantaloons

Zigzag all the edges.

Stitch the centre seams at the front and back.

Stitch the inside leg seams.

Fold down the ends of the legs by 6mm ($\frac{1}{4}$in) and attach the lace*.

8

Petticoat

This petticoat is very simple to make, and it will look best if you use a thin, white cotton, such as broderie anglaise. The petticoat has a casing for elastic at the waist and is decorated with tucks and a lace frill.

Variation If you have some pretty patterned material, use this design to make a light summer skirt.

Summer skirt

Cut a piece of thin material: small – 60 x 17cm (24 x 6$\frac{1}{2}$in); medium – 75 x 20cm (30 x 8in); large – 80 x 23cm (31$\frac{1}{2}$ x 9in).

Zigzag round all the edges.

Stitch the rectangle together down the centre back.

Turn up the bottom edge 1cm ($\frac{1}{2}$in) all round, lay the top edge of the lace behind it, with the frill hanging beneath the hem, and stitch the hem and the lace together from the right side.

Make one or two darts in the top of the skirt, then stitch a casing* at the waist, about 15mm ($\frac{3}{4}$in) deep, and pull the elastic through.

Nightdress 🧸🧸

Use a knitted fabric for this nightdress, which is fastened at the back with Velcro. Use lockstitch or small zigzag stitches for the whole pattern unless otherwise indicated.

Use the templates on page 66 to cut two backs, one front and two sleeves.

Stitch the centre back together to the point marked on the pattern. Fold back the rest of the seam by 1cm (1/2in) to each side and stitch.

Stitch the shoulder seams.

Work a row of close zigzag stitches around the bottom edge of the sleeves, about 1cm (1/2in) in from the edge. The material should be stretched while you sew, so that the edge has a wavy effect afterwards. Trim the edges neatly.

Stitch the sleeves to the front and back.

Stitch the underarm and side seams.

Zigzag around the bottom edge of the dress in the same way as the sleeve edges.

Fold down the edge of the neckline by about 6mm (1/4in) all the way round, and attach a lace* frill with ordinary stitching. Be careful not to stretch the edge of the neckline while you sew.

Attach a Velcro strip* as a fastening.

Variation 1 Stitch elastic in the sleeves. Ruffle the front with a little piece of elastic sewn on the wrong side of the front. Decorate it with a satin ribbon.

Variation 2 Decorate the bodice with a broad piece of lace, attaching the ends firmly but taking just a few stitches to hold the lace in position across the nightdress front. Trim the neckline and hem with lace.

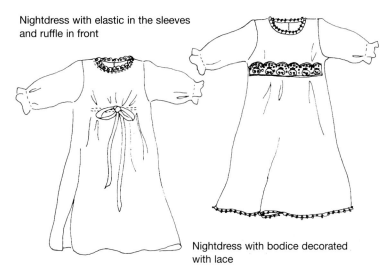

Nightdress with elastic in the sleeves and ruffle in front

Nightdress with bodice decorated with lace

Opposite
Dressing gown (page 12); Nightdress (page 10); Pantaloons (page 8); Dressing gown (page 12)

Dressing gown 🧸🧸🧸

The dressing gown can be made from towelling or velvet. All the edges are bound with satin ribbon or bias binding, and the seam allowance throughout is 1cm (1/2in).

Use the templates on page 68 to cut one back, two fronts, two sleeves and two pocket patches.

Zigzag stitch all the edges except the bottom edge, front edges and cuffs.

Attach the sleeves to the fronts and back. Stitch a 2cm (3/4in) hem at the cuffs and work three rows of stitching from the right side as decoration.

Use the ribbon or tape to make two small loops for the belt. Cut two lengths: small – 6cm (21/4in); medium – 7.5cm (3in); large – 8cm (31/4in). Fold the ribbon, wrong sides together, and join the short ends together. Turn to the right side, close the open edge and stitch the loops to the back, as indicated on the pattern.

Edge the top of the pocket patch with ribbon or bias binding*, fold over the sides and bottom of the pocket patch by 1cm (1/2in) and tack in place. Stitch the pockets to the fronts where marked on the pattern.

Stitch the underarm and side seams together. Make sure that the belt loops are pushed through to the right side before you stitch the side seams.

Beginning at the centre back of the neck, edge the front edges and hem with a long strip of ribbon or bias binding*.

Cut a piece of fabric for the belt: small – 55 x 31/2cm (211/2 x 11/4in); medium – 75 x 5cm (291/2 x 2in); large – 80 x 6cm (311/2 x 21/4in). Fold down all edges to the wrong side by 6mm (1/4in) and tack in place. Fold the belt lengthwise, wrong sides facing, and stitch together along the edges. Alternatively, use a length of cord or ribbon as a belt.

Dressing gown with bias binding or ribbon fastening (left) and with loops and toggles (right)

Variations Shorten the length of the dressing gown so that it reaches the doll's hips. Use lengths of ribbon or bias binding as a fastening or make two small loops for toggles or buttons.

12

T-shirt with set-in sleeves 🐻🐻

Make the T-shirt with an interlock fabric or stretch velvet. The whole garment is sewn with lockstitch or with small zigzag stitches, and the seam allowance is 1cm (½in) throughout, unless otherwise indicated.

Use the templates on page 66 to cut out two backs, one front and two sleeves.

Fold back the centre back seams by 1cm (½in) and stitch with ordinary stitches.

Change to lockstitch and stitch the shoulder seams.

facing, pin, then tack the band to the neck edge of the T-shirt, easing it over the shoulder seams and round to the back. The band can be easily extended to fit the neckline if necessary. Stitch on the band, allowing a 6mm (¼in) seam.

Stitch the underarm and side seams. Zigzag around the bottom edge and turn up a hem of 1cm (½in).

Attach a Velcro strip* at the back as a fastening.

Attach the sleeves and hem the cuffs by 1cm (½in).

Cut out a piece of fabric, cutting across the grain of the material, for the neck band: small – 16 x 3cm (6¼ x 1¼in); medium – 19 x 4cm (7½ x 1½in); large – 21 x 4cm (8¼ x 1½in). Fold the piece lengthwise, right sides together, and stitch the short ends with a 6mm (¼in) seam allowance. Turn to the right side. Find the centre front and the centre of the neck band. With right sides

Short-sleeved T-shirt 🧸

This T-shirt, which is best made from a knitted fabric, like jersey, is very easy to make. It should be sewn with a 6mm (¼in) seam allowance, using lockstitch or small zigzag stitches.

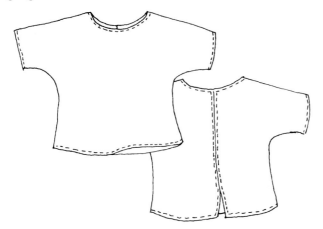

Use the templates on page 68 to cut one front and two backs.

Stitch the shoulder seams.

Turn up the cuffs.

Stitch the underarm and side seams.

Fold down the neckline by 6mm (¼in) and stitch.

Hem the T-shirt.

Fold over the edges of the backs and attach a Velcro strip* as a fastener.

Blouse with puffed sleeves 🧸🧸

Use plain or a patterned cotton material for this design. Stitch the blouse with a 1cm (½in) seam allowance throughout, and use Velcro for the fastening.

Use the templates on page 70 to cut out one front, two backs, two sleeves and four collars.

Zigzag all the edges.

Stitch the shoulder seams.

Turn up the cuffs.

Cut a length of elastic, slightly shorter than the width of the cuff. Zigzag stitch it to the wrong side, 2cm (¾in) from the edge of the cuff, stretching the elastic while you stitch so that the sleeve is ruffled.

(cont'd on page 16)

Opposite
Dress with pin tucks (page 34); Braid-trimmed jacket (page 36); Skirt (page 41); Cardigan (page 51); Pleated trousers (page 18)

Work a gathering thread* at the top of each sleeve and ease the gathers so that the sleeves fit neatly into the shoulder openings. Stitch the sleeves in place.

Stitch the side and underarm seams in one pass.

Iron interfacing to two of the collar pieces. With the collar pieces right sides facing, stitch along the curved edge, taking a seam allowance of 6mm ($^1/_4$in).

Turn the collars to the right side and press.

Stitch the collars to the neckline, with a 6mm ($^1/_4$in) seam allowance, so that the curved edge is facing to the front. Press the seam and stitch from the right side.

Hem the blouse.

Fold over the edges of the back pieces and attach the Velcro strip*.

Blouse with long sleeves

Blouse with lace collar

Variation 1 Instead of a collar, stitch a gathered lace frill to the neckline and also, if wished, to the cuffs.

Variation 2 The blouse can be made with long sleeves; simply lengthen the sleeve template to fit your doll.

16

Culottes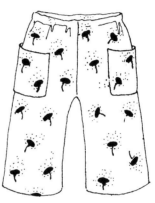

These culottes are very easy to make. They have an elastic waistband and are designed to be mid-calf length. Use a cotton fabric in light, cheerful colours and patterns. The seam allowance is 1cm (½in) throughout, unless otherwise indicated.

Use the templates on page 64 to cut two fronts and two backs.

Variation Cut two large pockets from the same material and two pieces, the same size, from lining fabric or another thin material. With right sides together, stitch the pocket and lining together, leaving an opening to turn the pocket out.

Turn the pocket out and press.

Stitch the pockets to the trousers.

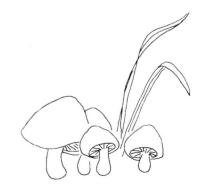

Culottes with pockets

Zigzag all the edges.

Stitch the centre front and back seams.

Stitch the inside leg and side seams.

Turn up a hem of 1cm (½in) on both legs.

Fold down the waist by 2cm (¾in) and make a casing*. Leave a small opening through which you can insert the elastic. Measure a length of elastic to fit around the doll's waist and thread it through the casing. Stitch the ends together.

Pleated trousers 🧸🧸

The trousers have four pleats at the front and are shaped at the back. They can be made from lightweight cotton or chintz. The seam allowance is 1cm (½in) throughout, unless otherwise indicated.

Use the templates on page 72 to cut two backs, two fronts and one waistband.

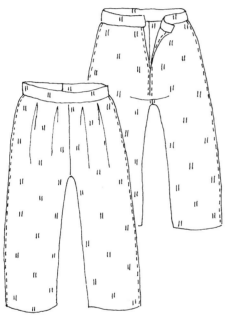

Zigzag all the edges.

Stitch the back pieces together from the crotch to the point marked on the pattern. Fold back the seam by 1cm (½in) on each side and sew.

Stitch the centre front seam together.

Stitch the inside and outside leg seams.

Try the trousers on the doll and make two small pleats in each front piece so that the trousers fit. Tack or pin the pleats to the waistband edge so that they stay in place while the waistband is attached.

Measure the waistband so that it fits around the doll's waist, adjusting the length if necessary. Fold the waistband lengthwise, right sides facing, and stitch the short ends, with a 6mm (¼in) seam allowance. Turn to the right side. With right sides facing, attach the waistband to the waist edge of the trousers. Turn under the inside edge and slip stitch or overstitch in place to hide the raw edges.

Attach a Velcro strip* as a fastening.

Hem the legs.

Bermuda shorts (left) and "pirate" trousers (right)

Variation 1 To make Bermuda shorts, shorten the legs so that they reach to the doll's knees. Stitch as above.

Variation 2 Make "pirate" trousers by shortening the legs so that they reach to just below the doll's knees. Stitch the side seams almost to the hem, but leave the last centimetre or so of the hem open. Fold under and press the seams. Stitch the opening all the way round. Turn up the trousers and stitch the hem.

Opposite
Trousers with bib (page 22); Skirt with bib (page 28); Trousers with bib (page 22); Dress with puffed sleeves (page 32)

Baby trousers

The broad ribbed waist of these trousers means that there is no need for any fastening. Use cotton or, if you have some, velvet, and if you do use velvet, there is no need to zigzag around the edges, because the whole design is sewn with lockstitch or small zigzag stitches. The seam allowance is 6mm (¼in) throughout.

Use the templates on page 82 to cut two trouser pieces.

Stitch ribbing* around the bottom edge of the legs, varying the depth according to size: small – 3cm (1¼in); medium – 4cm (1½in); large – 5cm (2in).

With right sides facing, stitch together the inside leg seams.

With right sides together, pin and stitch the centre seam in one pass, from centre front to centre back.

Measure the doll's waist and cut a piece of ribbing to this measurement, to a width of 6cm (2¼in) for a small doll, 8cm (3¼in) for a medium doll and 10cm (4in) for a large doll. Stitch the short ends together then fold the ribbing in half lengthwise.

Use pins or tacking stitches to divide both the ribbing and the waist of the trousers into four equal parts. Pin the ribbing to the waist, distributing the trouser fabric evenly. Stitch the ribbing to the trousers.

Measure the doll from waist to waist over the shoulders. Cut two identical pieces of fabric or ribbing to this size to a width of 4cm (1½in) for a small doll, 5cm (2in) for a medium doll and 6cm (2¼) for a large doll.

Fold the fabric or ribbing in half lengthwise and, with a 6mm (¼in) seam allowance, stitch along the long edge. Turn the straps right side out and press.

Stitch the straps at the back on the inside of the broad ribbing.

Attach pieces of Velcro strip to the other end of the straps and to the inside front of the ribbing.

Dungarees

A striped cotton fabric is ideal for this design, but you can use any cotton material. The seam allowance is 1cm (½in), unless otherwise indicated.

Use the templates on page 74 to cut two fronts, two back and one piece for the straps.

Zigzag all the edges.

Place one pair of front and back pieces together, right sides facing, and stitch the side and leg seams. Repeat with the other pair.

With right sides facing, pin then stitch the centre seam from top front to top back.

Turn up hems around the trouser cuffs and sew.

Fold over 6mm (¼in) around the angle of the back and the underarms, and stitch in place. Fold over 6mm (¼in) across the straight top edge of the front, neaten the corners and stitch.

Cut a strap: small – 25 x 2.5cm (10 x 1in); medium – 27 x 3cm (10½ x 1¼in); large – 30 x 4cm (12 x 1½in). Turn in 6mm (¼in) along each long edge and stitch down. Press.

Fold the strap in half to form a V-shape, neatly pressing the angles flat, and stitch it to the point at the centre back. If you wish, stitch a decorative square on the right side.

Add an iron-on motif to the front or attach an appliqué decoration.

If the trousers are too large around the waist, stitch a short length of elastic under the arms.

Attach press studs to the front bib and to the ends of the straps.

Use denim and decorate with overstitched seams.

Variation The same design can be used to make working dungarees from an old pair of denim jeans, which you can then decorate with pockets and overstitching worked with a contrasting colour thread.

Trousers with bib 🧸🧸🧸

The complete trousers have bib and straps, with ruffles edged with satin ribbon and stitched to the straps. The design can, however, be varied in a number of ways, according to the elements you choose to include. Use cotton or chintz or a similarly lightweight fabric. The seam allowance throughout is 1cm (¹/₂in), unless otherwise indicated.

Use the templates on page 76 to cut two trouser pieces, two trouser cuffs, one waistband, one bib, two straps and two ruffles.

Zigzag all the edges.

Begin with the trousers. Make seven to nine small tucks in the bottom edge of each leg. Make sure that the cuffs are the appropriate width for the length of the trouser legs, and ease the tucks at the bottom edge of the trousers to fit the cuff. With right sides together, stitch a trouser cuff to each trouser leg. Press and turn up a hem on the bottom edge of the trouser cuff of 1cm (¹/₂in).

Stitch the centre of the back to the point marked on the pattern. Fold back the remainder of the seam to each side and stitch down. Stitch the inside leg seams.

Make two pleats, each about 1.5cm (³/₄in) deep, in both front pieces. Tack them, adjusting the fit so that the trouser waist measurement corresponds to the length of the waistband and the doll's waist. If the trousers are too big make more or larger pleats, or make two small pleats in the back pieces; if necessary, shorten the waistband. If the trousers are too tight, make the pleats smaller and lengthen the waistband.

Fold 1cm (¹/₂in) of the short ends and one long side of the waistband towards the wrong side and stitch. With right sides facing, stitch the raw long edge of the waistband to the trousers. Turn the band up, press in position and overstitch the lower edge from the right side.

Make the straps. Fold over 1cm (¹/₂in) of both long edges and overstitch. Fold over 1cm (¹/₂in) of the top edge of the bib and stitch. Place the straps so that they overlap the sides of the bib by 1cm (¹/₂in) and stitch in position.

Trim the outside edge of the ruffles with ribbon or bias binding*. Run a gathering thread along the straight, inside edge. Gather the ruffles until they are about 3cm (1¹/₄in) shorter than the straps. Place the ruffles under the straps by about 1cm (¹/₂in), positioning them so that the midpoint of the ruffles matches the midpoint of the straps. Tack, then stitch the ruffles in place.

With both right sides upwards, place the bib behind the waistband, overlapping by about 1cm (¹/₂in). Tack in place, then work a row of stitches along the top edge of the waistband, holding the bib at the front and the straps at the back in position as you work around the band.

Attach a Velcro strip* as a fastening.

Note Some variations on this basic pattern are included on page 24, and some alternative ideas for decorating the bib are shown on pages 60–61.

Opposite
Baby trousers (page 20); Skirt with straps (page 29); Romper suit (page 42)

Variation 1 This version of the basic pattern is made with elastic in the legs but the ruffles are omitted.

Amend the template by increasing the length of the legs by the depth of the separate trouser cuffs. Stitch as explained on page 22, except for the trouser legs. Instead of attaching the cuffs, make a casing* at the end of each leg and pull through a length of elastic. The bib in this version has been trimmed with lace*, and the straps are sewn on behind the bib. (See the colour illustration on page 19.)

Variation 2 This version uses only the basic trousers and straps. Try making this version with the cuffs, waistband and straps in a different colour from the rest of the trousers. A tiny patterned fabric and plain trousers would look very pretty.

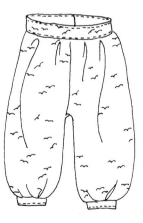

Variation 3 The trouser pattern can be used on its own to make a pair of roomy, comfortable trousers. (See the colour photograph on page 27.)

Shorts

The shorts, which have elastic around the waist, are made with turn-ups. Linen or a good strong cotton would be ideal for these. A seam allowance of 1cm (¹/₂in) is used throughout.

Use the templates on page 64 to cut two fronts and two backs.

Zigzag all the edges.

Stitch the centre front and back seams.

Stitch the inside leg and side seams.

Fold over the waist by 2cm (³/₄in) and make a casing*. Measure a length of elastic to fit the doll's waist, and pull it through the casing.

Turn the shorts the wrong way out and fold up the trouser legs by the following amount: short – 3cm (1¹/₄in); medium – 4cm (1¹/₂in); large – 4cm (1¹/₂in). Stitch in place from the wrong side. Turn to the right side. Find the midpoint of the turn-up and pull the outer layer of the material upwards until the turn-up is as deep as you wish. Hold in place with a couple of small stitches. Press.

Hem

Fold

Note Depending on the material used, this pattern can be used without the turn-ups to make boxer shorts or swimming trunks. The length of the leg can be adjusted as required, and the legs can be trimmed with tape or bias binding* in a contrasting colour or simply turned up by 1cm (¹/₂in) and hemmed.

The same pattern used for boxer shorts

25

Skirt

The skirt is simple and easy to stitch. It consists only of a long piece of material and a waistband. The measurements given will make a very full skirt, which will look very pretty in a light patterned cotton. The seam allowance is 1cm (1/2in) throughout, unless otherwise indicated.

Cut out a rectangle of your chosen fabric: small – 72 x 16cm (28¼ x 6¼in); medium – 85 x 19cm (33½ x 7½in); large – 90 x 21cm (35½in x 8¼in). Measure the doll's waist and cut a waistband to fit, remembering to add the seam allowance, and to a depth in proportion to the skirt: small – 6cm (2¼in); medium – 6cm (2¼in); large – 7cm (2¾in).

Zigzag all the edges.

Fold the waistband in half lengthwise, right sides together. Stitch the short ends, with a seam allowance of 6mm (¼in). Turn to the right side.

Work two gathering threads* in the top of the skirt piece. Pin, then stitch the centre back from the bottom edge to at least half way up. Gather the skirt until it is 2cm (1in) longer than the waistband. Tie a knot in the ends of the gathering threads when it is the right size. Fold over 1cm (½in) on each side of the seam opening at the back and stitch in position.

With right sides facing, stitch the waistband to the top of the skirt. Remove the gathering threads and slip stitch or overstitch the waistband on the inside to hide all raw edges.

Attach a Velcro strip* as a fastening.

Skirt with tucks and lace trim

Variation 1 Before you join the back seam, stitch two parallel tucks in the skirt and trim the hem with lace*.

Skirt with gathered flounce

Variation 2 Use a length of the same material to make a flounce. Stitch it to the hem and seam with coloured ribbon.

Opposite
Dress with puffed sleeves (page 32); Bikini top (page 30); Skirt (page 26); Blouse with puffed sleeves (page 14); Petticoat (page 9); Jacket (page 36); T-shirt (page 13); Trousers (page 24)

Skirt with bib 🧸🧸🧸

Make this skirt, which is fastened at the back with Velcro, from a pretty lightweight cotton or a similar fabric. The straps and waistband have to be cut to fit the individual doll (see below), and the seam allowance is 1cm (½in) throughout, unless otherwise indicated.

Use the templates on page 76 to cut out one skirt piece (see below), one waistband, one bib, two straps and two ruffles.

Cut out a rectangle of fabric for the skirt: small – 72 x 16cm (28¼ x 6¼in); medium – 85 x 19cm (33½ x 7½in); large – 90 x 21cm (35½ x 8¼in). Measure your doll's waist, and cut out a waistband to fit, adding 1cm (½in), and to a depth in proportion to the doll: small – 6cm (2¼in); medium – 6cm (2¼in); large – 7cm (2¾in).

Note The ruffles can be finished with a simple hem, as here, in which case you should add 1cm (½in) to the pattern on the rounded edge. Alternatively, you can bind the edges of the ruffle with ribbon or bias binding, when you should use the measurements indicated on the templates.

Follow the instructions on page 26 for stitching the skirt.

Fold over 1cm (½in) along the long edges of both straps and stitch down. Fold over both side edges and the top edge of the bib by 1cm (½in) and stitch. Stitch the straps to the bib, placing the straps in front of or behind the bib, as you prefer.

Fold over the curved edge of the ruffles by 6mm (¼in) and press. Fold over a further 6mm (¼in) and tack, then stitch the edge. Run a gathering thread* along the straight edge, and gather the ruffle until it is about 3cm (1¼in) shorter than the straps. Tack, then stitch the ruffles to the straps.

With both right sides up, place the bib behind the waistband, overlapping by about 1cm (½in). Stitch the bib to the waistband and stitch the straps to the back of the skirt.

Attach a Velcro strip* as a fastening.

Skirt with stitched detail

Variation Make the skirt out of a stiffer material and omit the ruffles. Use a contrasting thread to overstitch the seams.

Note Some alternative ways of decorating the bib are included on pages 60–61.

Skirt with straps

You could use cotton or velvet for this skirt. If you use velvet, use lockstitch or small zigzag stitch for all seams. If you use cotton, zigzag all edges first. The broad ribbed waistband means that there is no need for any fastening. The seam allowance is 6mm ($\frac{1}{4}$in) throughout.

There is no template for the skirt. Begin by measuring your doll's waist and from the waist to the knee (which will determine the length of the skirt).

Cut out a rectangle of fabric that is twice the waist measurement and the depth of the skirt plus a seam allowance at top and bottom.

Cut a piece of ribbing that is equal in length to the doll's waist measurement; the width will vary according to the size of your doll: small – 6cm ($2\frac{1}{4}$in); medium – 8cm ($3\frac{1}{4}$in); large – 10cm (4in). Stitch the short ends of the ribbing together, then fold it in half lengthwise, wrong sides facing.

Stitch the two short ends of the skirt fabric together to form the centre back seam. Turn up and stitch the hem.

Divide the ribbing and the skirt into four equal sections, using pins to mark the divisions. With right sides facing, pin, then tack the skirt to the ribbing, arranging the fabric evenly around the ribbing. Stitch in place, then turn the ribbing over the raw edges and overstitch or slip stitch in place on the inside.

Measure the doll from waist to waist over the shoulders. Cut two identical strips of ribbing to this measurement; the width will vary according to your doll: small – 4cm ($1\frac{1}{2}$in); medium – 5cm (2in); large – 6cm ($2\frac{1}{4}$in).

Fold the ribbing in half lengthwise, right sides facing and stitch along the long edge. Turn to the right side and press.

Stitch on the straps to the inside back of the waistband. Attach pieces of Velcro to the other ends of the straps and at the inside front of the waistband.

If you wish, decorate the front of the waistband with an iron-on motif or two tiny buttons.

Variation Use a lightweight patterned fabric to make a pretty summer skirt.

Bikini top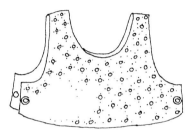

You could make this little top from cotton, chintz or a similar light fabric. It is fastened with two small press studs under the arms.

Use the templates on page 70 to cut one front and one back.

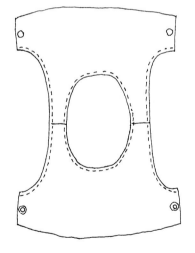

Zigzag all edges with small zigzag stitches.

Fold back the sleeve and neckline by 6mm (¹/₄in), tack, stitch and press. Fold up the bottom edges by 1cm (¹/₂in), stitch and press.

Fold back both side seams of each piece by 1cm (¹/₂in), stitch and press.

Stitch the shoulder seam together, allowing a 1cm (¹/₂in) seam.

Stitch a press stud to the side seams or, if you prefer, attach small pieces of Velcro.

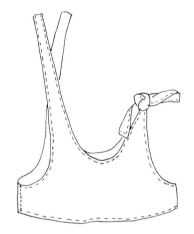

Variation If you lengthen the shoulders of both the front and back pieces and stitch the sides seams, the top can be fastened by knotting the shoulder straps.

Opposite
Culottes (page 17); T-shirt (page 13); Dungarees (page 21); Blouse with puffed sleeves (page 14); Sun hat (page 52); T-shirt (page 13); Pleated trousers (page 18)

Dress with puffed sleeves 🧸🧸🧸

This pretty party dress can be made with any small-patterned cotton fabric. It has extra lace and ribbon decorations, and is made with a 1cm (½in) seam allowance throughout.

Use the templates on page 63 to cut out one front, two backs, two sleeves and one skirt (see below).

Zigzag all the edges.

Stitch the shoulder seams together, press open the seams and overstitch from the right side.

Hem the cuffs. Stitch a piece of elastic 2cm (¾in) from the cuff, stretching the elastic while you sew so that the cuff will be gathered.

Run a gathering thread* around the top edge of each sleeve, and gather the fabric so that it fits evenly into the armhole. Pin, tack, then stitch the arms in position.

Stitch the underarm and side seams together.

Cut out a skirt to fit your doll: small – 64 x 16cm (25¼ x 6¼in); medium – 72 x 22cm (28¼ x 8½in); large – 78 x 24cm (31 x 9½in). Stitch the centre back seam, leaving open 5cm (2in) at the top.

Run a gathering thread* along the top edge of the skirt and distribute the folds of the fabric so that the skirts fits the bodice. Stitch the pieces together.

Fold over and press 6mm (¼in) along the seams at the back and attach a Velcro strip*.

Hem the skirt.

Work a gathering thread in a piece of lace trimming and pull it up so that it fits neatly around the neck. With wrong sides facing, stitch the lace in place. Turn the lace to the front and overstitch around the top of the neck to hold the lace in position. Finish by stitching narrow ribbon around the bodice seam.

32

Variation 1 Stitch on a simple collar instead of lace and make the bodice from a contrasting colour. See the pattern for the blouse on page 14 for the collar.

Variation 2 Stitch wide lace around the bodice and armhole seams. Fasten a length of narrow ribbon around the neck.

Variation 3 Shorten the sleeves; see the blouse on page 14.

Variation 4 Stitch two parallel bands of ribbon or ricrac braid around the hem and decorate the bodice with braid or narrow lace.

Dress with pin tucks

Use a lightweight cotton fabric with a small flowery pattern for this dress. It would look equally pretty in fine needlecord with a trim of velvet ribbon. The dress is decorated with pin tucks on the bodice. The seam allowance is 1cm (½in) throughout.

Use the templates on page 78 to cut one front, two backs, two sleeves and one neck band.

Zigzag all the edges.

Make four or five pin tucks* in the shoulder of each side of the front. Make one or two pin tucks in the back pieces, adjusting the fit so that the shoulders match. Stitch the front and back pieces together at the shoulder seams.

Turn up the cuffs. If you wish, make a pin tuck* 1cm (½in) from the cuff edge.

Stitch the sleeves to the back and front pieces.

Stitch the underarm and side seams together.

Stitch the centre back seam from the hem to the point marked on the pattern. Press back the unstitched opening and attach a Velcro strip* for the fastening.

With right sides facing, stitch together the short ends of the neck band. Turn to the right side. With right sides facing, pin, tack and stitch the neck band to the front and back pieces. Turn the neck band over the raw edges and overstitch or slip stitch in place. Alternatively, bind the neck edges with bias binding*.

Hem the skirt and stitch a tuck* 2cm (¾in) up from the hem.

Decorate by attaching a bow to the front.

Variation The same design can be used for a winter dress made of fine needlecord, decorated with velvet ribbon. Vary the length of the sleeves if you wish; see page 32.

Opposite
Hat and scarf (page 53); Coat (page 45); Rainwear (page 48); Jacket (page 44); Pleated trousers (page 18); Ski wear (page 46); Tote bag (page 55)

Jacket 🧸

This jacket can be made with an interlock fabric or with something more robust like velvet. The front edges and cuffs are decorated with two rows of stitching. There is no fastening, and all the seams are sewn with lockstitch or small zigzag stitch. The seam allowance is 1cm (½in) throughout.

Use the templates on page 80 to cut out one back, two fronts, two front sleeves and two back sleeves.

Stitch a front and back piece of each sleeve together. Repeat with the other sleeve.

Stitch the sleeves to the front and back pieces of the jacket.

Hem the cuffs, then stitch the side and underarm seams.

Turn back the neckline by 1cm (½in) and overstitch from the top. Work a second row of stitching close to the first.

Fold over the front edges by 1cm (½in) and overstitch from the top. Work a second row of stitching close to the first.

Braid-trimmed jacket 🧸🧸

This version of the same basic jacket is made with velvet and trimmed with satin ribbon. All the seams are sewn with lockstitch or small zigzag stitches, with a seam allowance of 1cm (½in) throughout.

Use the templates on page 80 to cut out one back, two fronts, two front sleeves and two back sleeves.

Follow the instructions above for stitching the sleeves to the front and back pieces.

Bind the cuffs with ribbon or bias binding*.

Stitch the side and underarm seams.

Beginning at the centre back, bind the neck and front edges with a long piece of ribbon or bias binding.

Jogging clothes

This easy pattern can be adapted to make all kinds of clothes, and it is suitable for different types of fabric. Use small zigzag or lockstitch for all seams, so there is no need to zigzag the edges of the pieces. The seam allowance is 6mm ($\frac{1}{4}$in) throughout.

Use the templates on page 82 to cut two trousers, one front, two backs and two sleeves.

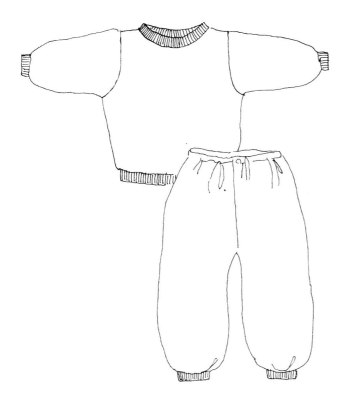

Trousers

Cut two lengths of ribbing, varying the size according to your doll: small – 12 x 6cm ($4^{3}/_{4}$ x $2^{1}/_{4}$in); medium and large – 16 x 7cm ($6^{1}/_{4}$ x $2^{3}/_{4}$in). Stitch the ribbing* to the trouser legs.

Stitch the inside leg seams.

Turn one leg inside out and place it inside the other, right sides facing. Stitch the seam from centre back to centre front. Turn to the right side.

Stitch a casing* around the waist and thread through a length of elastic.

Top

Stitch the shoulder seams.

Cut two pieces of ribbing, varying the size to fit your doll: small – 9 x 5cm ($3^{1}/_{2}$ x 2in); medium – 11 x 7cm ($4^{1}/_{4}$ x $2^{3}/_{4}$in); large – 12 x 7cm ($4^{3}/_{4}$ x $2^{3}/_{4}$in). Stitch the ribbing* to the cuffs.

Stitch the sleeves to the front and back pieces.

Stitch the underarm and side seams together.

Cut a piece of ribbing for the neck: small – 14 x 5cm ($5^{1}/_{2}$ x 2in); medium – 16 x 6cm ($6^{1}/_{4}$ x $2^{1}/_{4}$in); large – 16 x 6cm ($6^{1}/_{4}$ x $2^{1}/_{4}$in). Stitch the ribbing* to the neck opening of the sweater.

Cut a piece of ribbing for the waistband: small – 24 x 6cm ($9^{1}/_{2}$ x $2^{1}/_{4}$in); medium – 32 x 7cm ($12^{1}/_{2}$ x $2^{3}/_{4}$in); large – 35 x 8cm ($13^{3}/_{4}$ x $3^{1}/_{4}$in). Stitch the ribbing* to the bottom edge of the sweater.

Fold back the seam at the back by 1cm ($\frac{1}{2}$in) and attach a Velcro strip*.

If you wish, add an iron-on decoration to the front.

Note This pattern can also be used for pajamas; use a lightweight jersey fabric and cut the ribbing from the same material.

Variation 1 Appliqué a number to the front to make a track suit top.

Variation 2 Use a contrasting colour for the top of the sleeves. Join two pieces of fabric together before cutting around the template.

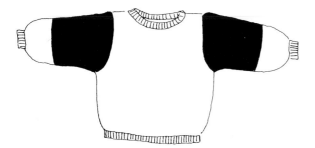

Variation 3 The pattern can be adapted to using several different colours. Make sure that the fabrics are all more or less the same weight.

Variation 4 Personalize the top by appliquéing or embroidering the doll's name.

Opposite
Sun hat (page 52); T-shirt (page 13); Shorts (page 25); Dungarees (page 21); Jogging clothes (page 37)

Track suit

The track suit is made with two different but coordinating shades of lightweight cotton. The trousers have elasticated legs and waist and the top has a two-colour collar. Zigzag all raw edges. The seam allowance is 6mm (¼in) throughout.

Use the templates on page 82 to cut out two trousers, one front, two backs and four collars (two pieces in each colour).

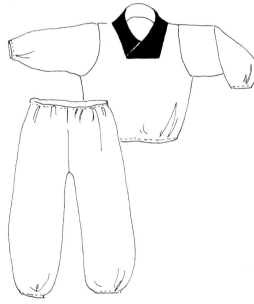

Trousers
Stitch both inside leg seams.

Make a casing* at the bottom of each trouser leg and thread through the elastic.

Turn one leg to the right side, and put it in the other leg, with right sides facing. Stitch the seam from centre back to centre front. Turn to the right side.

Make a casing* around the waist and thread through the elastic.

Top
Stitch the shoulder seams and stitch the sleeves to the armholes.

Stitch the underarm and side seams.

Make a casing* at the cuffs and thread through the elastic.

Stitch part of the way up the centre back seam: small – 5cm (2in); medium – 7cm (2¾in); large – 8cm (3¼in). Attach a Velcro strip* to the opening for a fastening.

Take two matching collar pieces, in different colours, and place them with right sides facing. Stitch along the short seam at centre back and along the long top edge. Repeat with the other two pieces. Open both sections out and press.

Pin, then tack the first collar piece in position around the neck, right sides together, clipping the neckline and seams to ease the fit and reduce bulk. Stitch in place, beginning at the centre front, and stitching through the front of the collar and the neck. Repeat with the other collar piece, checking that it lies neatly over the first. Turn to the right side and fold under the inside edges. Overstitch or slip stitch in place to cover all raw edges.

Stitch a casing* around the waist and thread through the elastic.

Note You could use this pattern to make a leisure suit from velour or velveteen.

Blouson jacket and skirt 🧸🧸

The casual jacket and skirt have been made with jersey, and there are ribbed edgings at the collar, cuffs and waist, which means there is no need for a fastening. The seam allowance is 1cm (½in) throughout, unless otherwise indicated, and the seams should be worked with lockstitch or small zigzag.

Use the templates on page 90 to cut two fronts, one back, two sleeves and one skirt (see below).

Jacket

Stitch the shoulder seams.

Cut two pieces of ribbing, varying the dimensions according to your doll: small – 9 x 4cm (3½ x 1½in); medium – 11 x 6cm (4¼ x 2¼in); large – 12 x 6cm (4¾ x 2¼in). Stitch the ribbing to the cuffs*.

Stitch in the sleeves.

Stitch the underarm and side seams together.

Turn back the front opening by 6mm (¼in) on each side and press.

Measure the neckline and add 1cm (½in). Cut out a piece of ribbing to this length, varying the width to fit your doll: small – 4cm (1½in); medium and large – 5cm (2in).

Fold the ribbing in two lengthwise, right sides together, and stitch the short ends, with a seam allowance of 6mm (¼in). Turn to the right side.

With right sides facing, pin, then stitch the ribbing around the neckline, with a seam allowance of 6mm (¼in). Turn the collar up and turn under the long unstitched edge of the ribbing. Overstitch or slip stitch in place to cover all raw edges.

Make the waistband of the jacket by cutting a piece of ribbing: small – 32 x 4cm (12½ x 1½in); medium and large – 40 x 5cm (15¾ x 2in). Fold the ribbing, right sides together, in half lengthwise and stitch the short ends with a seam allowance of 6mm (¼in). Turn to the right side.

With right sides facing, pin then stitch the long edge of the ribbing to the bottom edge of the jacket. Turn under the unstitched long edge of the ribbing and overstitch or slip stitch in place at the back of the jacket, to hide all raw edges.

Skirt

Measure the doll's waist and the length from the waist to the knee. Cut out a rectangle of fabric that is twice the waist measurement and the depth of the skirt plus a seam allowance at top and bottom.

Cut out a piece of ribbing that is the length of the waist measurement; the width will vary according to your doll: small – 4cm (1½in); medium – 5cm (2in); large – 6cm (2¼in).

Take a gathering thread* along the top edge of the skirt. Distribute the fabric evenly before stitching on the ribbing*.

Stitch the seam at the centre back before hemming the skirt.

Note Instead of attaching ribbing to the skirt, make a casing* and thread through a length of elastic.

Romper suit 🧸🧸

This soft, roomy romper suit can be made from velvet or a stretchy fabric. It is fastened at the front with three press studs. Stitch with lockstitch or the smallest zigzag stitch and with a seam allowance of 1cm (¹⁄₂in) throughout.

Use the templates on page 84 to cut two fronts, two backs and two sleeves.

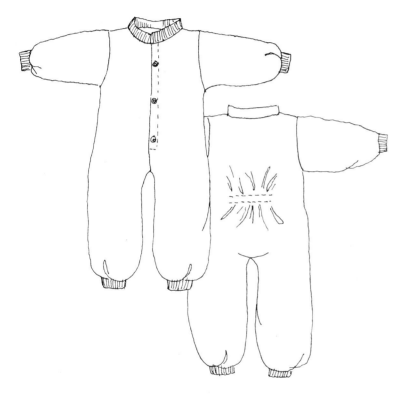

Stitch the shoulder seams.

Stitch in the sleeves.

Cut two pieces of ribbing for the cuffs: small – 4 x 8cm (1¹⁄₂ x 3¹⁄₄in); medium – 5 x 8.5cm (2 x 3¹⁄₂in); large – 6 x 9cm (2¹⁄₄ x 3¹⁄₂in). Stitch the ribbing to the cuffs*.

Stitch the underarm and side seams together.

Cut two pieces of ribbing for the trouser legs: small – 4 x 8cm (1¹⁄₂ x 3¹⁄₄in); medium – 5 x 9.5cm (2 x 3³⁄₄in); large – 6 x 10.5cm (2¹⁄₄ x 4¹⁄₄in). Stitch the ribbing to the trouser cuffs*.

Stitch the inside leg seams.

Turn one of the pieces to the right side and put it in the other, right sides facing and matching the edges. Stitch down the centre back seam up to the point marked on the pattern.

Fold under 1cm (¹⁄₂in) on each front piece and stitch.

Cut a piece of ribbing for the neckline, varying the depth according to your doll: small – 3cm (1¹⁄₄in); medium – 4cm (1¹⁄₂in); large – 5cm (2in). Pin, then stitch the ribbing* to the neckline.

Stitch on the press studs, making sure that you position the top and bottom parts of each stud accurately.

Turn the romper suit to the wrong side and stitch a small piece of elastic to the centre back, stretching the elastic as you stitch. If the romper suit is already a tight fit on your doll, omit the elastic.

Opposite
Jogging clothes (page 37); Track suit (page 40); Short-sleeved T-shirt (page 14); Denim dungarees (page 21)

Jacket

Make this jacket from a fairly robust fabric such as denim, quilted material or wool. It can be fastened with press studs or a strip of Velcro. The seam allowance is 1cm ($\frac{1}{2}$in), unless otherwise indicated.

Use the templates on page 86 to cut one back, two fronts, one collar, two pockets, two sleeve fronts and two sleeve backs.

Zigzag all the edges.

Stitch the back and front sleeve pieces together. Stitch the sleeves to the front and back pieces. Turn up a hem on the cuffs.

Stitch the underarm and side seams. Hem the jacket.

Fold the collar in half lengthwise, right sides facing, and stitch the short ends, with a 6mm ($\frac{1}{4}$in) seam allowance. Turn to the right side. Making sure that the centre of the collar is in the centre back of the jacket,

pin, then stitch the collar to the neck, right sides facing and with a seam allowance of 6mm ($\frac{1}{4}$in). Turn up the collar and press under the raw edge. Slip stitch the unstitched edge of the collar to the inside of the neck, making sure that all raw edges are neatly hidden.

Turn back the front facings. Overstitch the long front openings of the jacket. Ideally, the bottom facing should be stitched down by hand.

Fold over the top edge of the pockets by 1cm ($\frac{1}{2}$in) and sew. Fold over the rest of the pocket edges by 1cm ($\frac{1}{2}$in) and tack. Stitch the pockets onto the jacket.

Attach the press studs down the front opening or attach a Velcro strip*.

Coat

The coat is long and generously cut. It is fastened all the way down the front with press studs. Make it with a robust, fairly stiff fabric such as strong cotton, linen or wool, The seam allowance is 1cm ($\frac{1}{2}$in), unless otherwise indicated.

Use the templates on page 88 to cut one back, two fronts, two sleeve fronts, two sleeve backs, one collar and two pockets.

The coat is made up and stitched in the same way as the jacket on page 44.

The coat shown in the photograph on page 35 has facings and a collar lining made with a different coloured material, and the pockets are also lined. If you wish to do this, cut two extra pieces the same size as the facings, adding 1cm ($\frac{1}{2}$in) seam allowance to the edge of the facing, and an extra collar, adding an extra 1cm ($\frac{1}{2}$in) seam allowance.

With right sides facing, stitch the facings to the front sections of the coat (see the illustration) and turn over the original facing. Stitch as for the jacket.

Stitch the two collar pieces together before attaching the collar as for the jacket.

Cut out two pocket pieces of each colour material. Stitch them together in pairs, right sides facing and with a 6mm ($\frac{1}{4}$in) seam allowance. Leave a small opening to turn the pocket through. Stitch the opening by hand, press, then attach the pocket to the front of the coat, overstitch about 6mm ($\frac{1}{4}$in) in from the pocket edge.

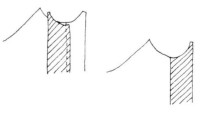

Attaching the coloured lining to the facing

45

Ski wear 🧸🧸🧸

If possible, use a weatherproofed cotton or a fabric like gabardine. The fastening is a Velcro strip, and if you can, try to find some Velcro the same colour as the fabric. The design has a lot of decorative stitching and other details, but these can be omitted if you wish. The seam allowance is 1cm (¹/₂in) throughout.

Use the templates on page 84 to cut two fronts, two backs, two sleeves, one collar (see below) and four strips (see below).

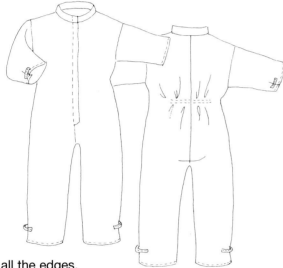

Zigzag all the edges.

Stitch the shoulder seams. Press the seams open and overstitch two rows of decorative stitching from the right side.

Stitch the sleeves to the armholes.

Turn up the cuffs and overstitch a row of stitching. Stitch two strips, each 6 x 2cm (2¹/₄ x ³/₄in), and attach pieces of Velcro to the strips and to the cuffs.

Stitch the sleeve and side seams together. Overstitch decorative stitching from the right side.

Hem the trouser legs. Cut two strips, each 6 x 2cm (2¹/₄ x ³/₄in), and attach them to the trousers with pieces of Velcro to match the sleeves.

Stitch the inside seams of the legs.

Turn one of the pieces to the right side and place it in the other, matching raw edges. Stitch down the back seam and up to the point marked on the pattern.

Make sure that the front edges overlap. Fold over the front edges by 1cm (¹/₂in) and attach a Velcro strip* right down the front opening. Stop the Velcro strip 6mm (¹/₄in) below the neckline.

Measure the neckline and cut a piece of material with this measurement plus a 1cm (¹/₂in) seam allowance; the width depends on the size of your doll: small – 5cm (2in); medium and large – 6cm (2¹/₄in).

Fold the collar in half lengthwise, right sides together, and stitch the short ends together with a 6mm (¹/₄in) seam allowance. Turn to the right side and press.

Attach the collar to the neckline as described for bias binding* and stitch decorative stitching from the right side. Attach a small length of Velcro at the front to fasten the collar.

If you wish, appliqué a badge or other decoration on the front or on one sleeve.

If the garment is very loose, stitch a piece of elastic on the wrong side of the back with zigzag stitch, stretching the elastic while you stitch. This can be omitted if the garment is a tight fit.

Opposite
Pierrot costume (page 49); Patterned sweater (page 50); Trousers (page 24); Blouson jacket and skirt (page 41)

Rainwear

The rainwear consists of a jacket with a hood and trousers with a bib. They can be made from thin, soft plastic material, which you can sometimes find in DIY stores, or from nylon. The seam allowance is 1cm (¹/₂in) throughout. Zigzag all edges before stitching.

Use the templates on pages 82 and 90 to cut one hood, one back, two fronts, two sleeves, two trousers, one bib and two straps (see below).

Jacket

Stitch the shoulder seams together.

Turn up the cuffs.

Stitch the sleeves into the armholes.

Stitch the underarm and side seams together.

Turn up and hem the jacket.

Stitch the hood together at the top and make a casing* around the front. Pull through a length of fine cord.

With right sides facing, position the neckline of the hood against the neckline of the jacket. Leaving 1cm (¹/₂in) unstitched at the beginning and end and, making sure that the cord can run freely, stitch the hood to the neck.

Fold over the front seams by 1cm (¹/₂in) and stitch in position.

Attach the press studs.

Variation You can easily make a raincoat using the same pattern and method as for the jacket on page 44. Simply adjust the length of the front and back so that they reach to the doll's knees. Remember to add a seam allowance, and turn up a hem around the bottom.

Trousers

Turn up the trouser legs.

Stitch the inside leg seams.

Turn one leg to the right side and put it inside the other leg, right sides facing and matching the raw edges. Stitch from centre back to centre front.

Fold over 1cm (1/2in) on the two short sides and one long side of the bib and stitch down.

With right sides facing up, place the bib just behind the front of the trousers, centring it over the centre seam. Turn over the top of the waist by 1cm (1/2in) and stitch the bib in position.

Pierrot costume

This costume is made from white linen or cotton and is decorated with three large pompons, made with different coloured wools. Stitch with a seam allowance of 1cm (1/2in) throughout.

Use the templates on page 84 to cut two backs, two fronts and two sleeves.

Zigzag all the edges.

Stitch the shoulder seams.

Stitch on the sleeves.

Turn up the cuffs.

Stitch the underarm and side seams together.

Turn up the trouser legs and sew.

Stitch the inside leg seams.

Turn one trouser leg to the right side out and put it inside the other leg, right sides together and matching raw edges. Stitch the seam down the back and up to the point marked on the pattern.

Fold over 1cm (1/2in) around the rest of the trouser edge and make a casing*. Thread a length of elastic through and stitch it firmly at both sides of the bib.

Measure the doll from back waist to the top of the bib over the shoulder and cut out two strips to this length, varying the width according to the size of your doll: small – 4cm (1 1/2in); medium and large – 5cm (2in). Fold over 6mm (1/4in) along each long side and stitch.

Attach the straps at the back of the waist and attach press studs to the bib and the straps at the front.

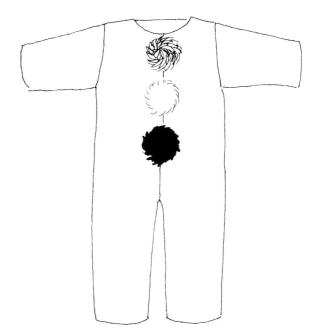

Fold over the neckline by 6mm ($\frac{1}{4}$in) and stitch it down. It will lie flatter if you nick the fabric up to the seam line.

Fold back 1cm ($\frac{1}{2}$in) down the front edges and sew.

Turn back the front openings, making sure that they overlap each other, and attach a Velcro strip* as a fastening.

Use different coloured wools to make three pompons and stitch them down the front, spacing them evenly.

Variation This pattern can be made as a clown's costume by using different colours – perhaps red and yellow – for the two halves. Stitch on a gathered collar as a ruff.

Patterned sweater 🐻🐻

Where three figures are given in the instructions, they refer to the three sizes – small/medium/large. You will need about 50g (2oz) cotton yarn and a small scrap of yarn in a contrasting colour; knitting needles sizes 2$\frac{1}{2}$ and 3.

Pattern Knit 2 rows plain in the main colour; thereafter knit every third row as follows: 3 stitches in the main colour, 1 stitch in the contrasting colour. Stagger the position of the contrasting stitches as shown in the illustration.

Front
Cast on 35/42/50 stitches on size 2$\frac{1}{2}$ needles in the main colour and rib (knit 1, purl 1) for 8 rows. Change to size 3 needles and cast on 4/6/8 stitches across the first row.

Knit straight up in the pattern until the knitting measures 8/10/11cm (3$\frac{1}{4}$/4/4$\frac{1}{4}$in). Shape the armholes by casting off 3,2/3,2,1/3,2,1 stitches at the beginning of the next rows. Then knit straight for 4/5/6cm (1$\frac{1}{2}$/2/2$\frac{1}{4}$in).

Put the central 8/10/12 stitches on a safety pin and finish each side in turn. Shape the neck by casting off 1 stitch at the beginning of the next 3 rows. Knit until the armhole measures 6/9/11cm (2$\frac{1}{4}$/3$\frac{1}{2}$/4$\frac{1}{4}$in). Cast off. Knit the other side in the same way.

Back

Knit as described for the front until the knitting measures 13/17/19cm (5/6¾/7½in). Put the central 8/10/12 stitches on a safety pin and finish each side in turn. Shape the neck by casting off 2 stitches then 1 stitch at the beginning of the next two rows. Cast off when the back and front pieces are the same length.

Sleeves

Cast on 26/30/34 stitches on size 2½ needles in the base colour and rib (knit 1, purl 1) for 8 rows. Change to size 3 needles and cast on 4/6/8 stitches across the first row. Knit plain, remembering to knit in the pattern. Cast on 1 stitch on each side every third row. Knit until the sleeve measures 10/12/14cm (4/4¾/5½in). Cast off 3/2/1 stitches at the beginning of the next 2 rows. Cast off the remaining stitches.

Cardigan 🧸

Instructions are for small/medium/large. You will need about 50g (2oz) mohair yarn or similar; knitting needles sizes 3 and 3½.

The cardigan is knitted in one piece, beginning with the back. Cast on 35/42/49 stitches on size 3 needles and

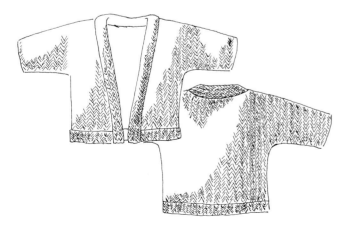

Stitch one shoulder seam together. Stitch the other shoulder 1cm (½in) in from the top of the arm seam. Stitch on the sleeves. Stitch the underarm and side seams.

Working from the right side, pick up 54/56/58 stitches from around neck, including the stitches on the safety pins, and rib (knit 1, purl 1) for 8 rows. Cast off in rib.

Stitch a Velcro strip* in the open shoulder as a fastening.

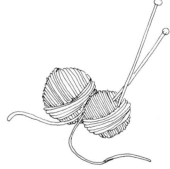

rib (knit 1, purl 1) for 6 rows. Change to size 3½ needles and knit 5cm (2in) straight in plain knitting. Cast on 1 stitch at the beginning and end of the next 3 rows.

Shape the sleeves by casting on 14/17/20 stitches at the beginning and end of the next row. Knit straight for a further 6/8/10cm (2¼/3¼/4in).

Shape the neck by casting off the central 13/15/17 stitches. Finish knitting each side in turn. Cast off 1 stitch at the beginning of every second row to shape the neck.

Work the front side. Knit 2/3/4cm (¾/1¼/1½in). Cast on 1 stitch on the neck side on each fourth row five times.

When the sleeves are 11/12/13cm (4¼/4¾/5¼in) deep, cast off 14/17/20 stitches, then cast off 1 stitch every other row three times.

Continue to knit the front until it is the same length as the back, Change to size 3 needles and rib for the next 6 rows. Cast off. Knit the other side to match.

Work the front edge by casting on 8/10/12 stitches on size 3 needles and rib (knit 1, purl 1) until the edge reaches right around the front, neck and down the other front of the cardigan's opening. Cast off and stitch the edging to the front opening.

Stitch the underarm and side seams.

Sun hat

The hat is made from linen or cotton. You can vary the design by overstitching the brim in a different colour or even by using different coloured fabrics for the brim and the crown. The seam allowance is 6mm ($\frac{1}{4}$in) throughout.

Use the templates on page 92 to cut four brim and six crown pieces.

Zigzag all the crown pieces.

With right sides facing, place two brim piece together and stitch the short edges together. Turn to the right side and press. Repeat with the other two brim pieces. Place the two brim pieces together, right sides facing, and stitch along the outside. Turn and press. Stitch rows of decorative stitches at intervals of about 1cm ($\frac{1}{2}$in).

Stitch the crown pieces together, then, with right sides facing, stitch the crown to the brim.

Lace collar

This loose collar can be used both with dresses and blouses, and it is very easy to sew.

Cut out an appropriate length of lace; it should be about twice as long as the neckline of the blouse or dress.

Run a gathering thread* along the top edge, draw it up and arrange the ruffles so that the collar fits the doll's neck.

Fold over the ends by 6mm ($\frac{1}{4}$in) and stitch. Attach a press stud.

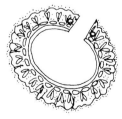

Hat and scarf 🧸

Dolls generally have proportionately large heads, so the pattern for the hat is rather large in relation to the other patterns in the book. Make it with ribbed fabric, with a seam allowance of 6mm (¹/₄in).

Note Make it look like a ski hat by stitching a decorative pattern on the front of the hat.

Variation Make the hat from fabric of two different colours so that the turned up section is a contrasting colour.

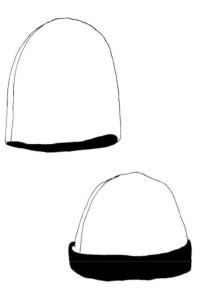

Scarf

Cut out two pieces of fabric as long and as wide as you wish.

With right sides facing, stitch along the two long edges and one short edge. Turn through to the right side.

Close the open end of the scarf by hand and press.

Variation Make the scarf from two different colours of ribbed material to make it look really smart.

Hat

Use the templates on page 92 to cut four hat pieces.

With right sides facing, stitch two of the hat pieces together along the long edge. Repeat with the other two pieces.

Place the pieces together, right sides facing, and stitch them together around the bottom, leaving about 3cm (1¹/₄in) open on one side.

Turn the hat right side out through the opening, and close the opening by hand.

Turn up the lower part of the hat to form a brim and press it in position.

53

Shoulder bag 🧸🧸

The bag is made from a remnant of flowered cotton material and edged with satin ribbon or bias binding. It is lined with a thin layer of wadding.

Use the templates on page 92 to cut two bag pieces and one piece of thin quilting.

Zigzag all edges.

Place the wadding between the two layers of material.

Place the satin ribbon on the short straight side. Stitch it on as described for attaching bias binding*.

Fold the bottom of the bag up. Pin, then tack ribbon all round the outside edge of the bag.

Make a strap out of the ribbon and attach it to both sides of the bag, just under the flap.

Stitch the binding* on all the way round.

Stitch a small piece of Velcro to the centre front and the inside centre flap. Stitch this by hand so that the stitches cannot be seen from the right side.

Tote bag

The tote bag is made with red cotton and has green corners. Alternatively, use a flowered cotton fabric with plain coloured corners. The seam allowance is 6mm ($^1/_4$in) throughout.

Use the templates on page 92 to cut two bag pieces and four corner pieces.

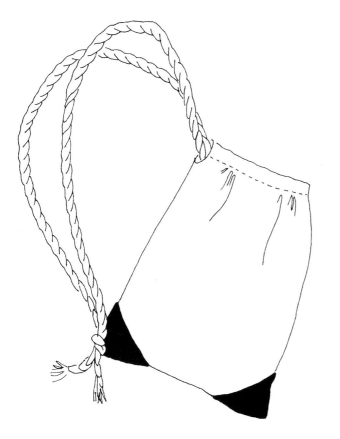

Zigzag all the edges.

Place two corner pieces, right sides facing, across the bottom corners of one bag piece. The angles should point upwards. Make sure the triangles will cover the bottom corners of the bag when they are turned down. Stitch both triangles along the long side. Fold down to cover the corner and press. Repeat with the other triangles and the other bag piece.

Place the two bag pieces together, right sides facing, making sure that the triangles are at the bottom of the bag. Pin the bag, then stitch along the two long sides and across the bottom, beginning 2cm ($^3/_4$in) from the top edge.

Press open the seams at the sides and fold down the top 1cm ($^1/_2$in) all round. Stitch to make a casing with an opening at one side.

Thread through a long piece of fine cord. Tie a knot at the end of the cord and hand stitch the knot to one of the corners.

Attaching a Velcro strip

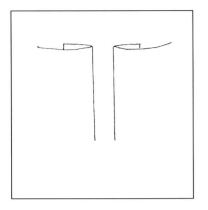

Fold back the seam allowance on both sides.

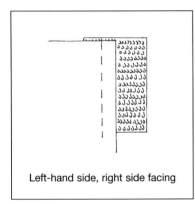

Left-hand side, right side facing

Place the piece of Velcro that has the small hooks behind the material so that half the strip protrudes.

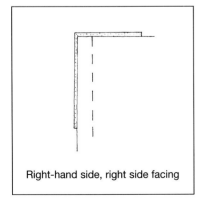

Right-hand side, right side facing

The other part of the Velcro, which is fluffy, is placed entirely behind the material so that the edge of the Velcro strip is flush with the edge of the seam.

Attaching lace

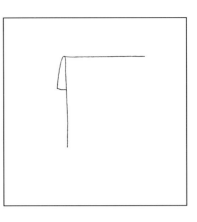

Fold over the edge of the garment.

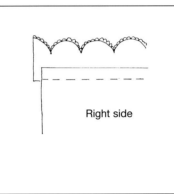

Right side

Place the lace a little bit behind the edge and, if you wish, tack in place. Stitch the folded fabric and the lace together from the right side.

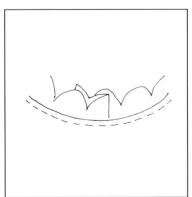

If the opening is curved or round – as with an armhole or neck – fold the lace back by about 1cm (½in) at the beginning and place the raw end behind this.

Attaching ribbed edgings

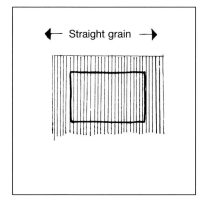

Always cut the ribbing across the grain to give greater elasticity.

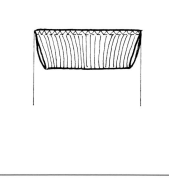

Stitch the ribbing to the fabric with lockstitch or small zigzag stitches, stretching the ribbing slightly while you work.

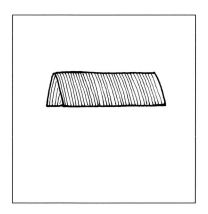

Fold the ribbing in half lengthwise.

Attaching bias binding

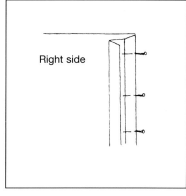

With right sides facing, position the edge of the opened-out tape so that it is flush with the edge of the fabric. Pin and tack in place.

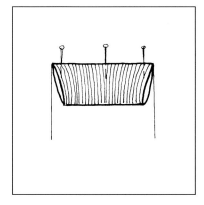

Begin by pinning the ribbing to the garment, right sides facing, placing pins at the ends and in the centre.

Stitch along the fold line of the bias binding.

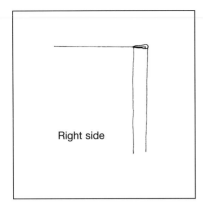

Fold the bias binding over the edge of the fabric and to the back and stitch it down by hand.

Right side

If you are covering sharply rounded corners, press the bias binding into shape with a hot iron before stitching it on.

Making a casing

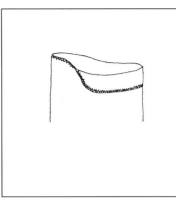

Zigzag the edge and fold it down, wrong sides together, by 1½–2cm (about ¾in).

Stitch along the lower edge, leaving a small opening through which the elastic or cord can be threaded. Attach the elastic to a safety pin or use a bodkin to thread the elastic through the casing. Close the opening by hand.

When you are making a casing in something large – like a pair of trousers – it is a good idea to make a row of stitching at the top of the waistband. Stitch all the way round, leaving the gap for the elastic in the lower row of stitches.

Stitching gathering threads

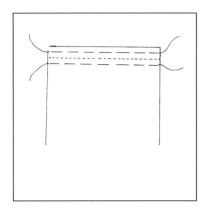

Adjust your sewing machine to the longest possible stitch. Work two rows of stitches, each about $^1/_2$–1cm ($^1/_2$in) from the seam line.

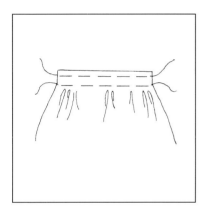

Pull the lower thread until the fabric is the desired length, making sure that the fabric is evenly distributed along the length. Fasten off the threads.

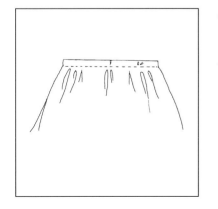

Stitch along the seam line, then carefully remove the gathering threads.

Making pin tucks

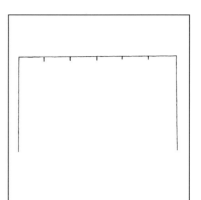

These little tucks are really vertical pleats. Use a ruler to mark the position of the top of each tuck on the fabric.

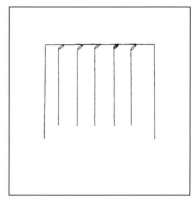

Fold the tucks in the fabric and press them. Do not crease the fabric beyond the tuck.

Use your machine to stitch each tuck.

Decorating bibs

Stitch some contrasting fabric to the bib and decorate it with coloured ribbon or tape.

Embroider the doll's name.

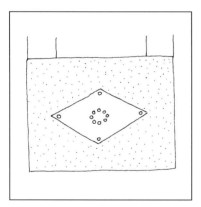

Cut out a geometric shape and appliqué it to the front of the bib.

Cut out a motif from a piece of curtain or furnishing fabric and appliqué it to the bib.

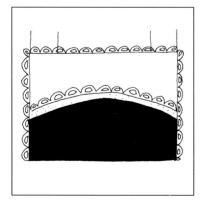

Attach lace around the edge of the bib or decorate the front of the bib with lace.

Some craft shops stock motifs that can be glued or stitched to fabric.

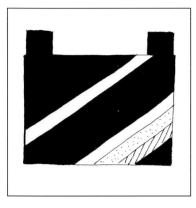

Stitch together lengths of ribbon and tape in a rainbow of colours to cover the front of the bib.

Exploit the possibilities of stitching the bib in front of as well as behind the straps.

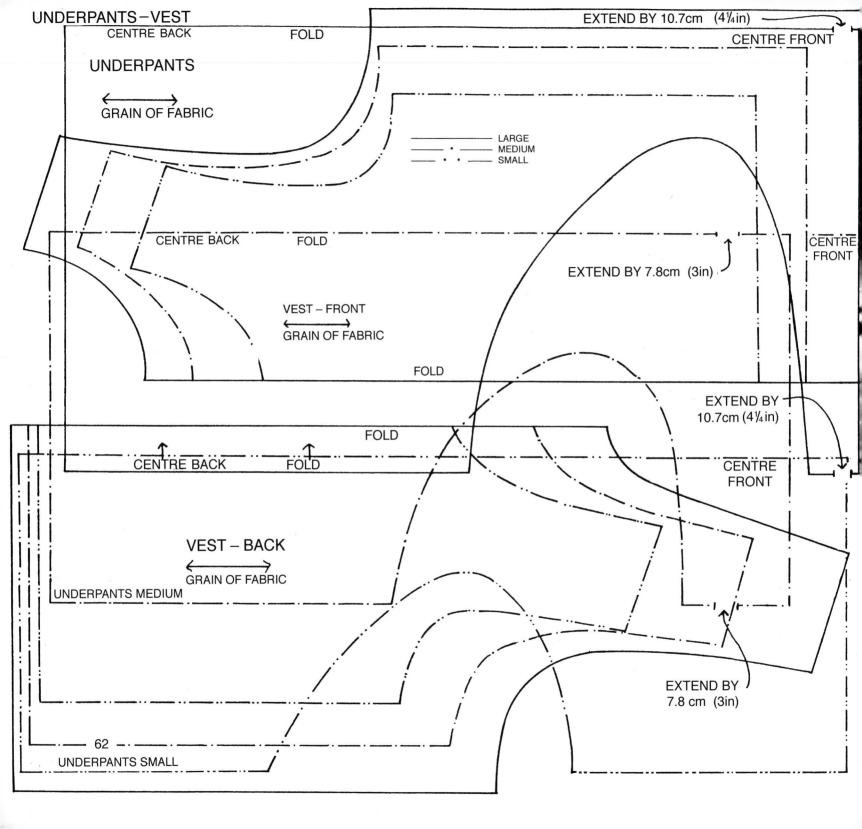

UNDERPANTS–VEST

CENTRE BACK   FOLD   EXTEND BY 10.7cm (4¼in)   CENTRE FRONT

UNDERPANTS

GRAIN OF FABRIC

———————— LARGE
—·—·—·— MEDIUM
—··—··—·· SMALL

CENTRE BACK   FOLD   CENTRE FRONT

EXTEND BY 7.8cm (3in)

VEST – FRONT
GRAIN OF FABRIC

FOLD

EXTEND BY
10.7cm (4¼in)

FOLD

CENTRE BACK   FOLD   CENTRE FRONT

VEST – BACK
GRAIN OF FABRIC

UNDERPANTS MEDIUM

EXTEND BY
7.8 cm (3in)

62

UNDERPANTS SMALL

DRESS WITH PUFFED SLEEVES

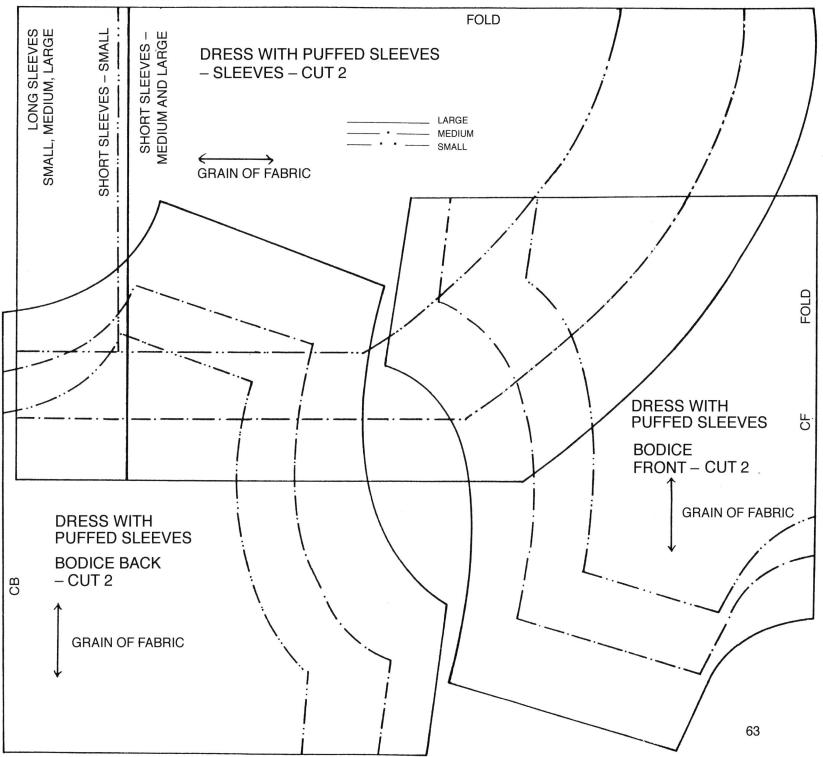

LONG SLEEVES
SMALL, MEDIUM, LARGE

SHORT SLEEVES – SMALL

SHORT SLEEVES –
MEDIUM AND LARGE

DRESS WITH PUFFED SLEEVES
– SLEEVES – CUT 2

LARGE
MEDIUM
SMALL

GRAIN OF FABRIC

FOLD

FOLD

CF

DRESS WITH
PUFFED SLEEVES

BODICE
FRONT – CUT 2

GRAIN OF FABRIC

CB

DRESS WITH
PUFFED SLEEVES

BODICE BACK
– CUT 2

GRAIN OF FABRIC

63

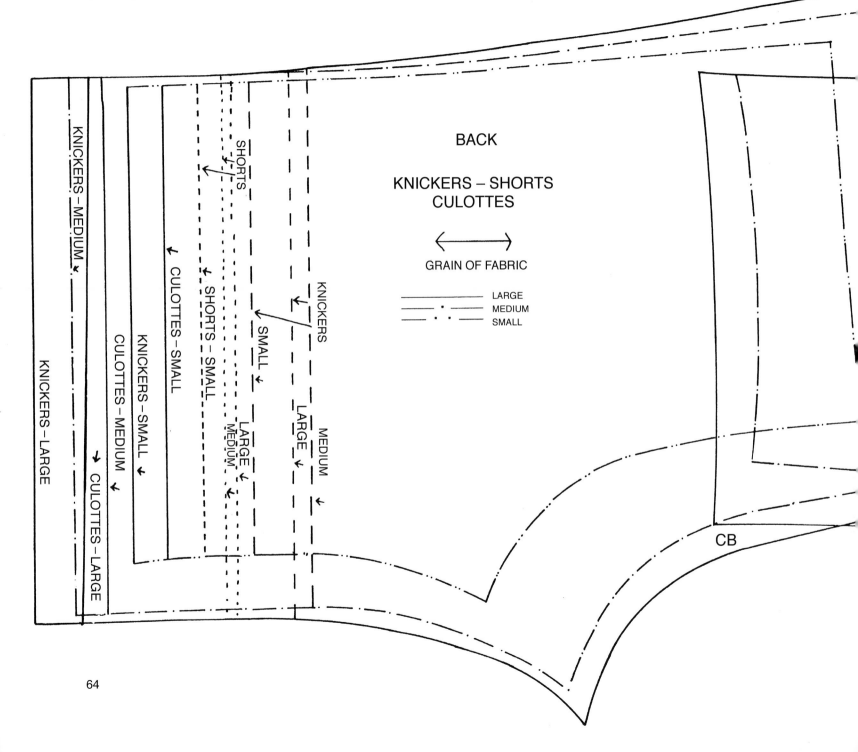

BACK

KNICKERS — SHORTS
CULOTTES

⟵⟶

GRAIN OF FABRIC

————————	LARGE
—— · —— · ——	MEDIUM
—— · · —— · · ——	SMALL

CB

KNICKERS — MEDIUM

KNICKERS — LARGE

CULOTTES — MEDIUM

CULOTTES — LARGE

KNICKERS — SMALL

CULOTTES — SMALL

SHORTS

SHORTS — SMALL

KNICKERS

SMALL

LARGE

MEDIUM

LARGE
MEDIUM

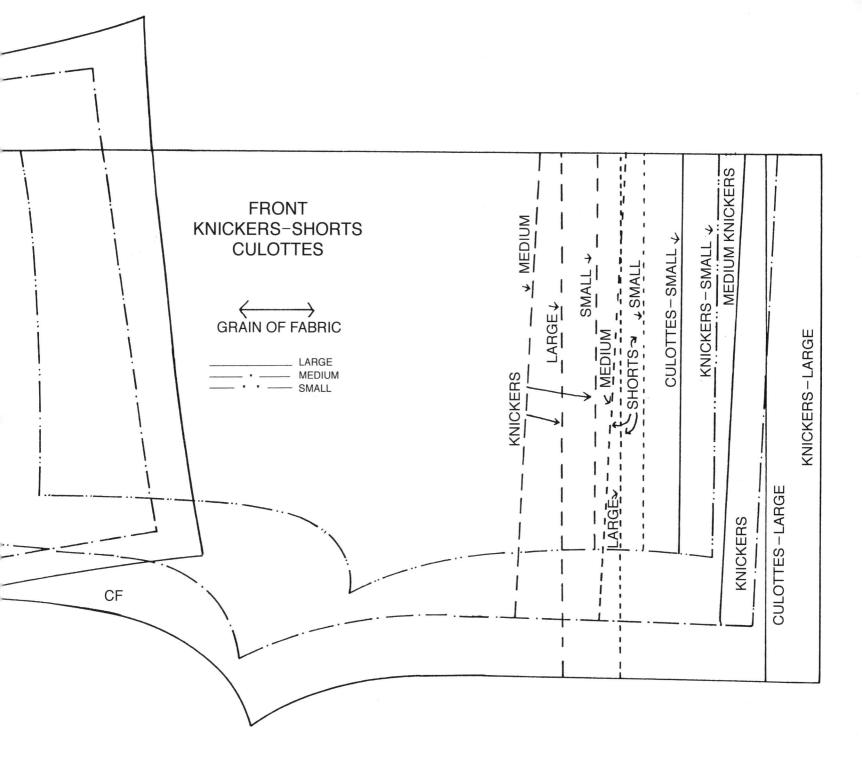

FRONT
KNICKERS-SHORTS
CULOTTES

GRAIN OF FABRIC

LARGE
MEDIUM
SMALL

KNICKERS

MEDIUM

LARGE

SMALL

MEDIUM

SHORTS

SMALL

LARGE

CULOTTES-SMALL

KNICKERS-SMALL

MEDIUM KNICKERS

KNICKERS-LARGE

KNICKERS

CULOTTES-LARGE

CF

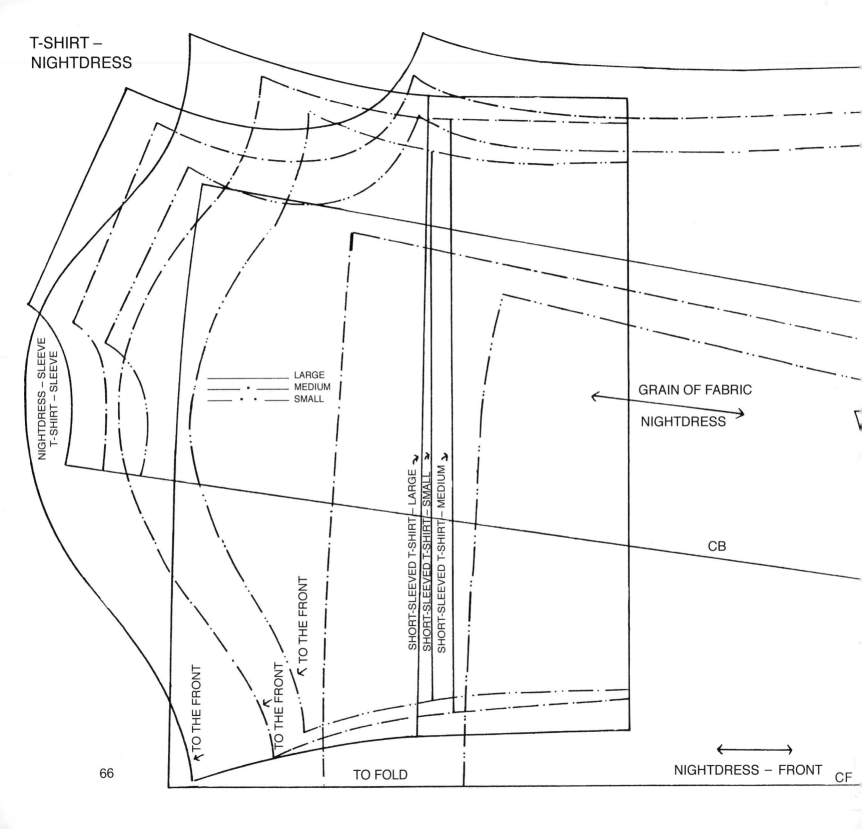

T-SHIRT –
NIGHTDRESS

NIGHTDRESS – SLEEVE
T-SHIRT – SLEEVE

LARGE
MEDIUM
SMALL

GRAIN OF FABRIC

NIGHTDRESS

SHORT-SLEEVED T-SHIRT – LARGE
SHORT-SLEEVED T-SHIRT – SMALL
SHORT-SLEEVED T-SHIRT – MEDIUM

CB

TO THE FRONT
TO THE FRONT
TO THE FRONT
TO THE FRONT

66

TO FOLD

NIGHTDRESS – FRONT

CF

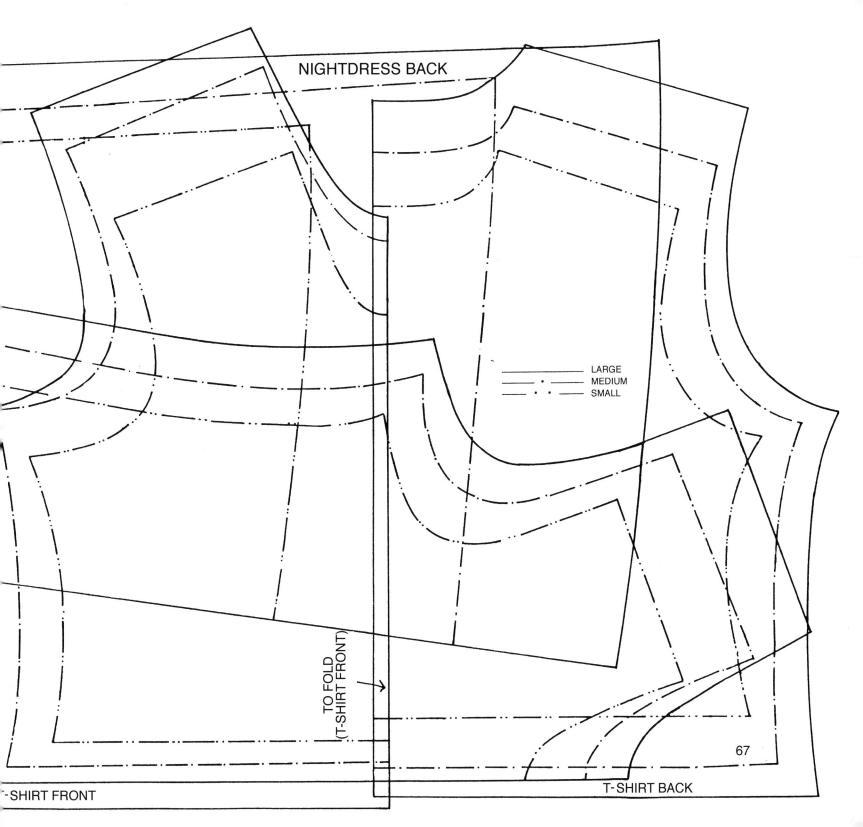

NIGHTDRESS BACK

LARGE
MEDIUM
SMALL

TO FOLD
(T-SHIRT FRONT)

T-SHIRT FRONT

T-SHIRT BACK

67

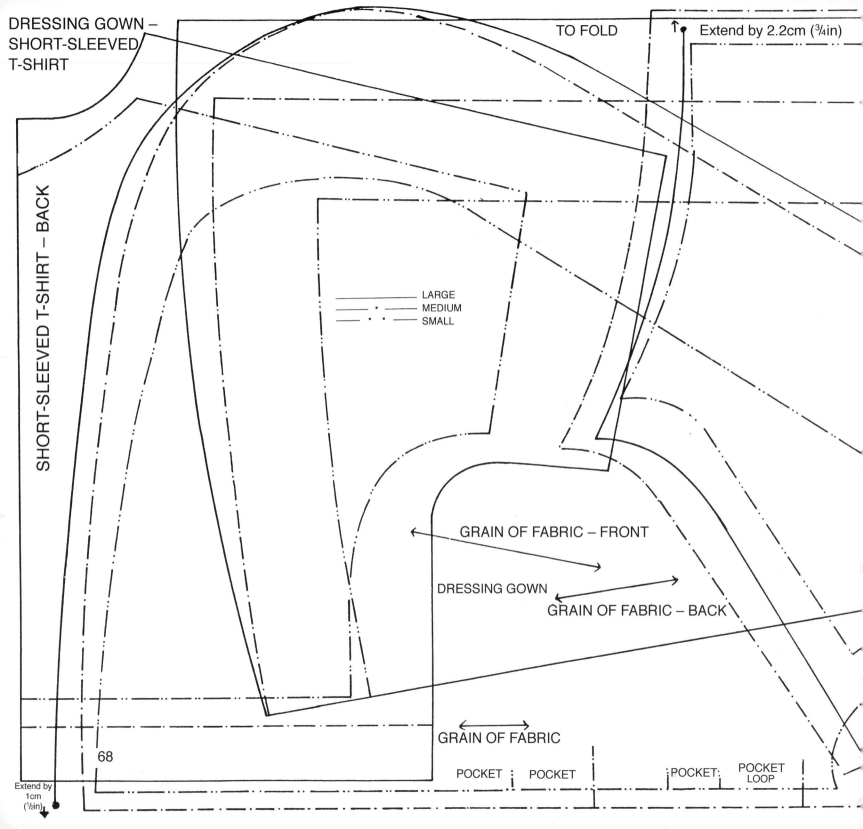

DRESSING GOWN –
SHORT-SLEEVED
T-SHIRT

TO FOLD

Extend by 2.2cm (¾in)

SHORT-SLEEVED T-SHIRT – BACK

LARGE
MEDIUM
SMALL

GRAIN OF FABRIC – FRONT

DRESSING GOWN

GRAIN OF FABRIC – BACK

GRAIN OF FABRIC

68

Extend by
1cm
(½in)

POCKET   POCKET   POCKET   POCKET
LOOP

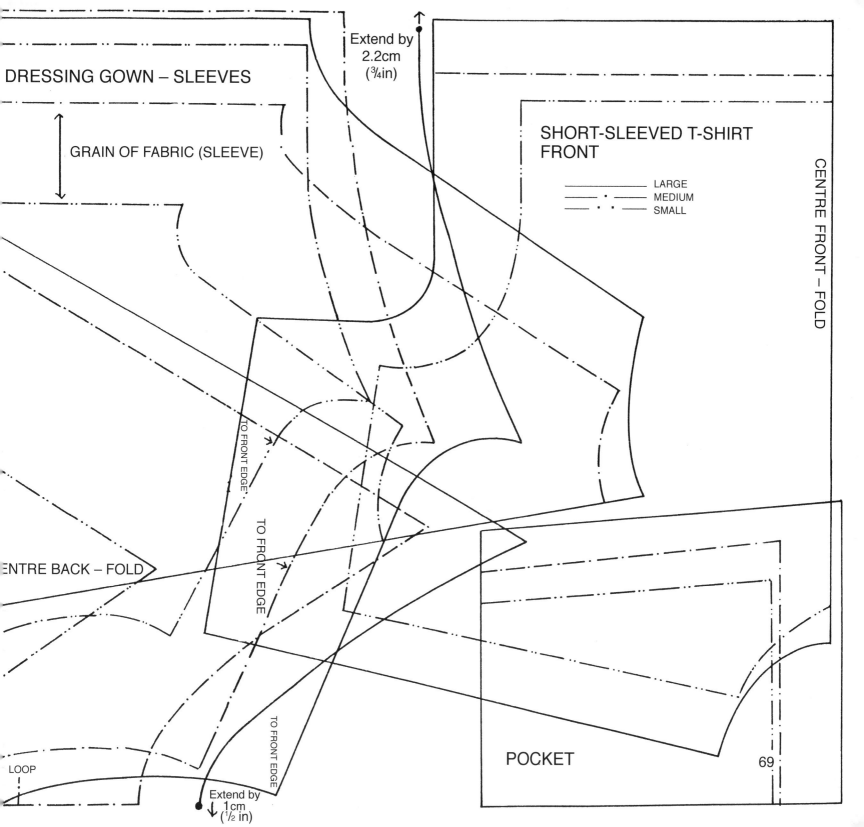

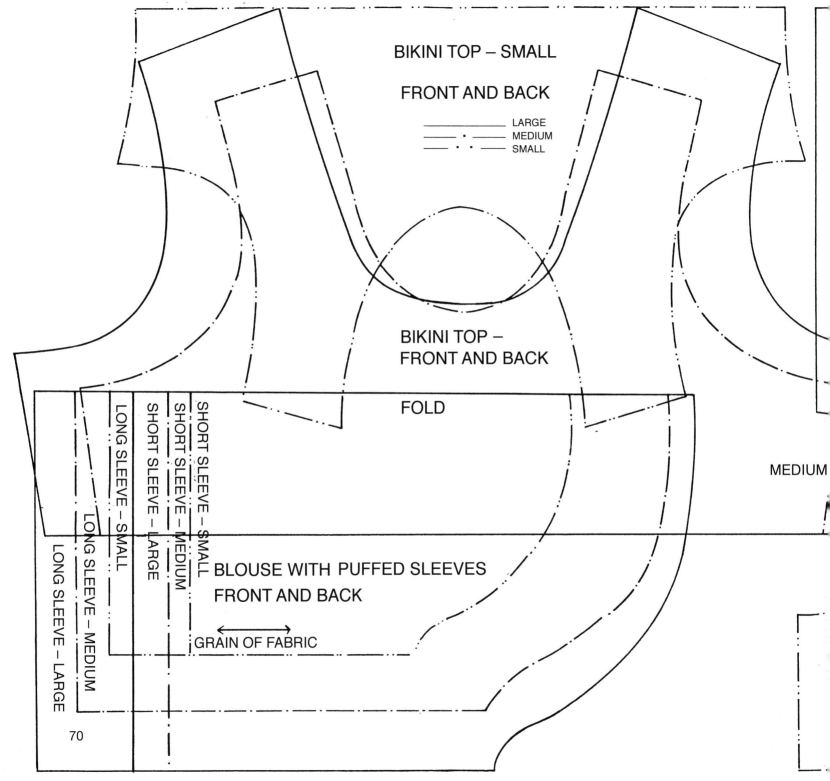

BIKINI TOP – SMALL

FRONT AND BACK

———————— LARGE
——·—·—·—— MEDIUM
——··—··—— SMALL

BIKINI TOP –
FRONT AND BACK

FOLD

MEDIUM

LONG SLEEVE – SMALL

LONG SLEEVE – MEDIUM

LONG SLEEVE – LARGE

SHORT SLEEVE – LARGE

SHORT SLEEVE – MEDIUM

SHORT SLEEVE – SMALL

BLOUSE WITH PUFFED SLEEVES
FRONT AND BACK

GRAIN OF FABRIC

70

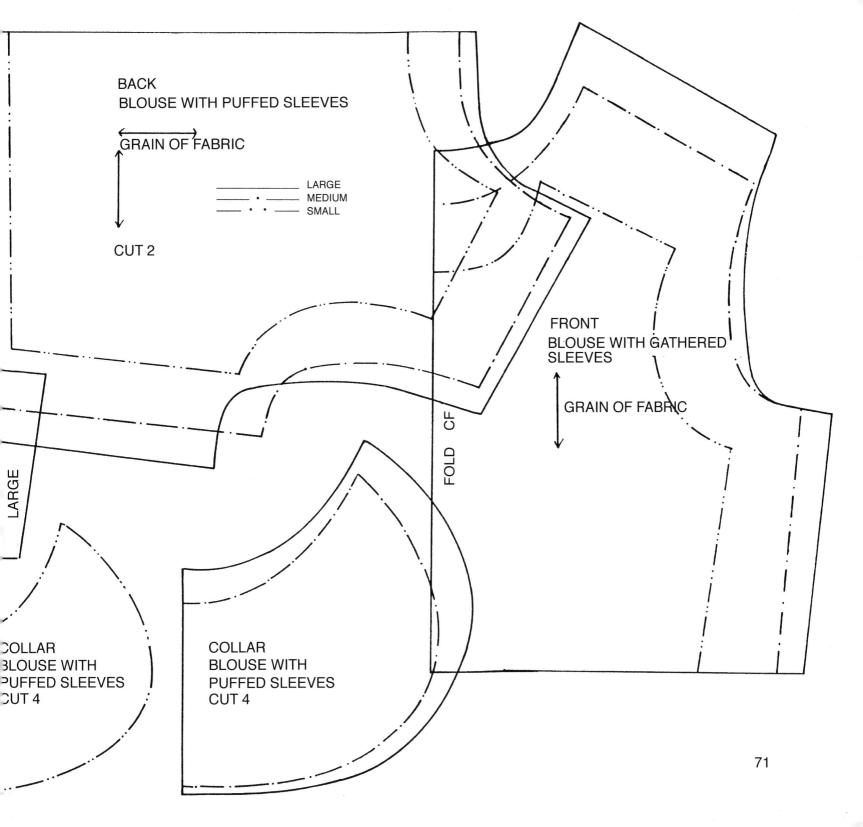

BACK
BLOUSE WITH PUFFED SLEEVES

GRAIN OF FABRIC

LARGE
MEDIUM
SMALL

CUT 2

FRONT
BLOUSE WITH GATHERED SLEEVES

GRAIN OF FABRIC

LARGE

FOLD CF

COLLAR
BLOUSE WITH
PUFFED SLEEVES
CUT 4

COLLAR
BLOUSE WITH
PUFFED SLEEVES
CUT 4

71

PLEATED TROUSERS

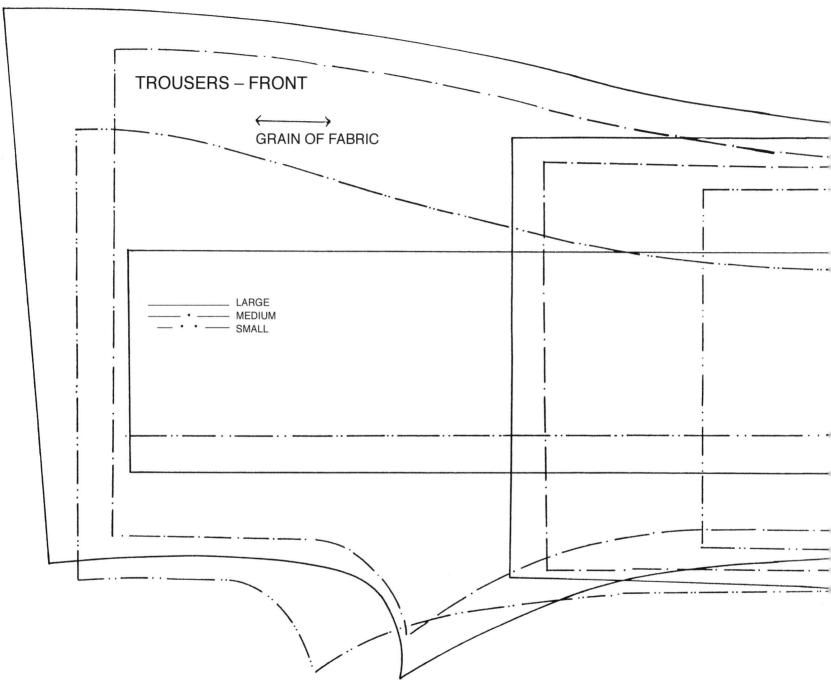

TROUSERS – FRONT

GRAIN OF FABRIC

——————— LARGE
——·——·—— MEDIUM
——··——··—— SMALL

72

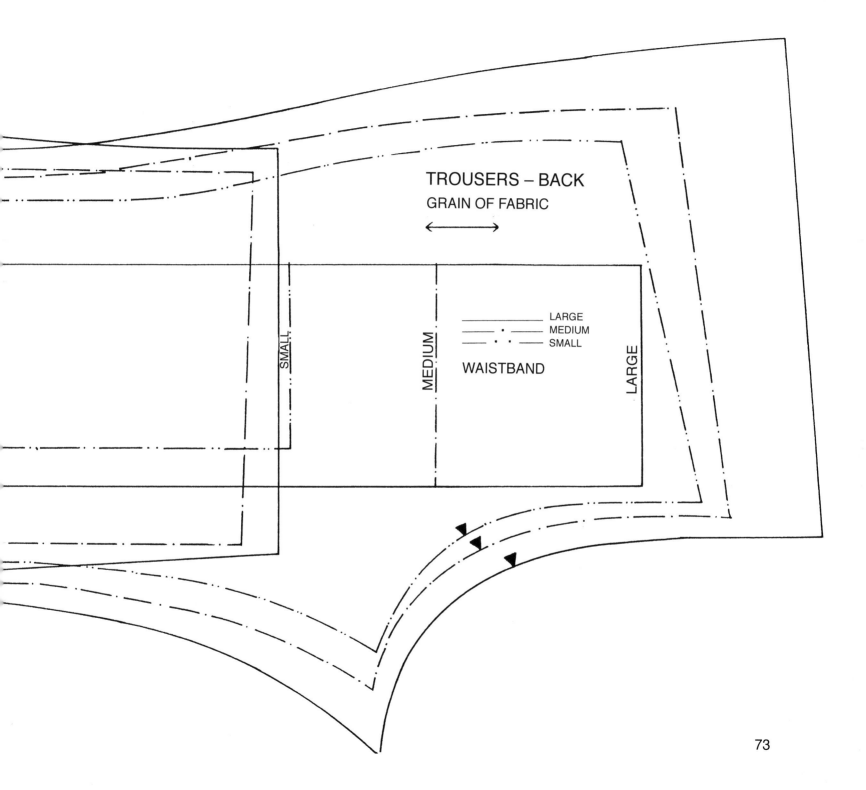

TROUSERS – BACK

GRAIN OF FABRIC

←——→

SMALL

MEDIUM

LARGE

WAISTBAND

——————— LARGE
——·——·—— MEDIUM
——··——··—— SMALL

73

DUNGAREES

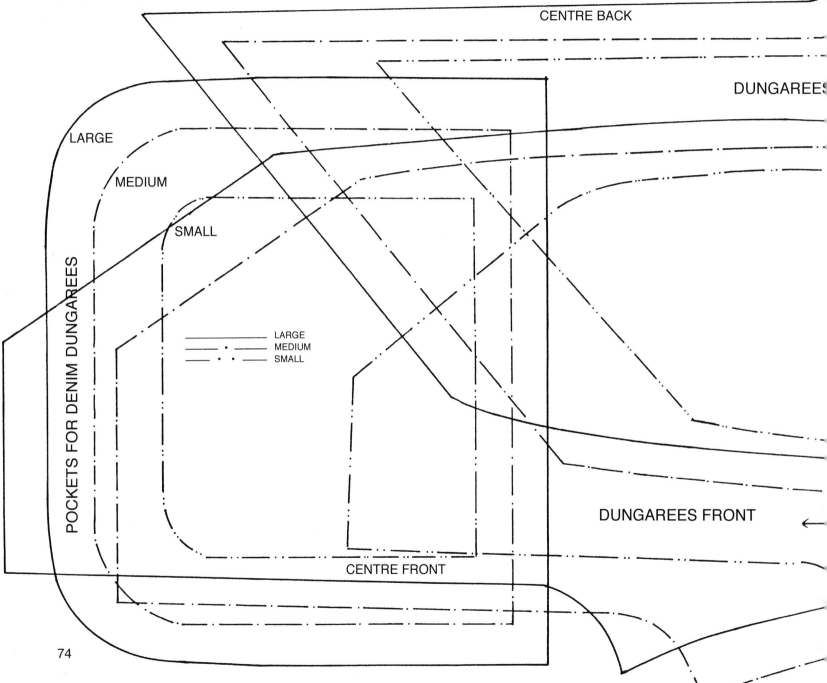

CENTRE BACK

DUNGAREES

LARGE

MEDIUM

SMALL

POCKETS FOR DENIM DUNGAREES

	LARGE
	MEDIUM
	SMALL

DUNGAREES FRONT

CENTRE FRONT

74

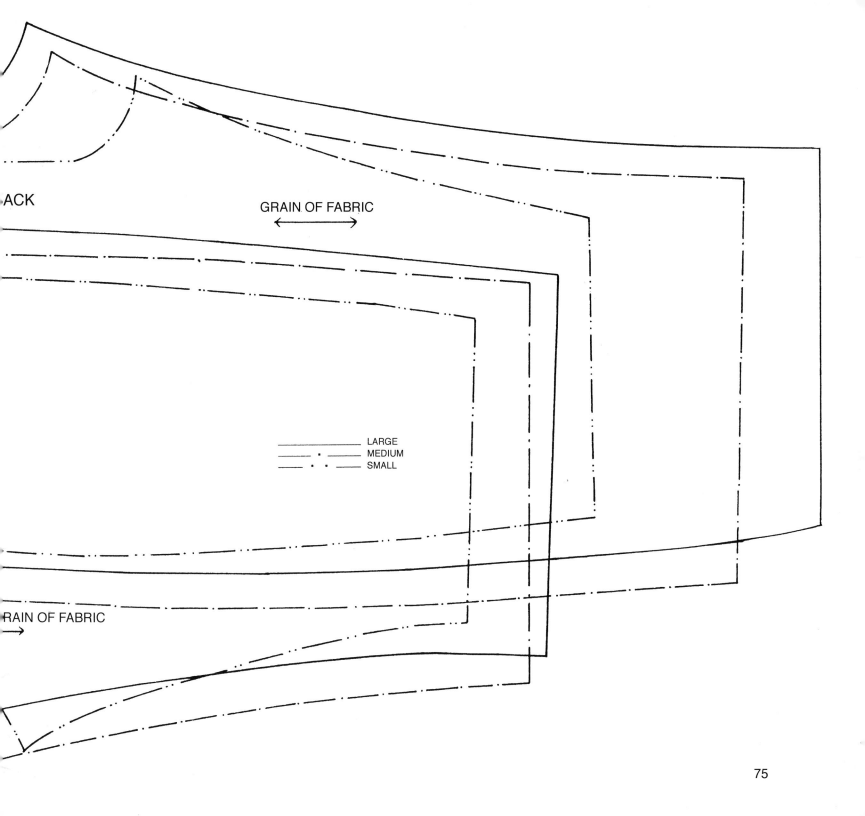

ACK

GRAIN OF FABRIC

LARGE
MEDIUM
SMALL

RAIN OF FABRIC

75

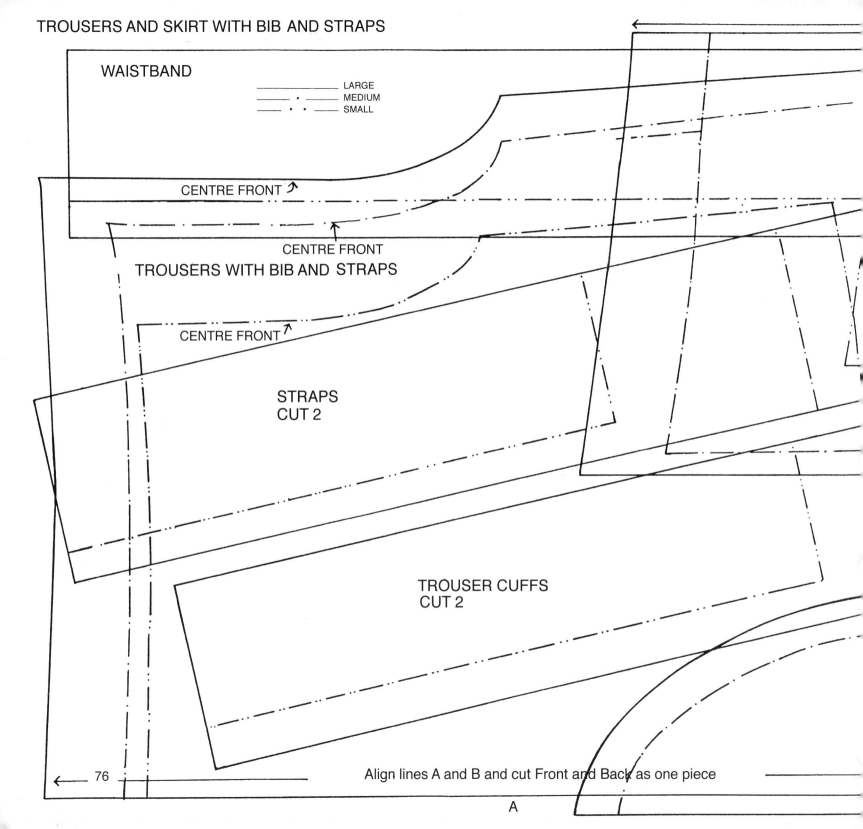

TROUSERS AND SKIRT WITH BIB AND STRAPS

WAISTBAND

_____ LARGE
_ _._ _ MEDIUM
····· SMALL

CENTRE FRONT ↗

CENTRE FRONT

TROUSERS WITH BIB AND STRAPS

CENTRE FRONT ↗

STRAPS
CUT 2

TROUSER CUFFS
CUT 2

← 76

Align lines A and B and cut Front and Back as one piece

A

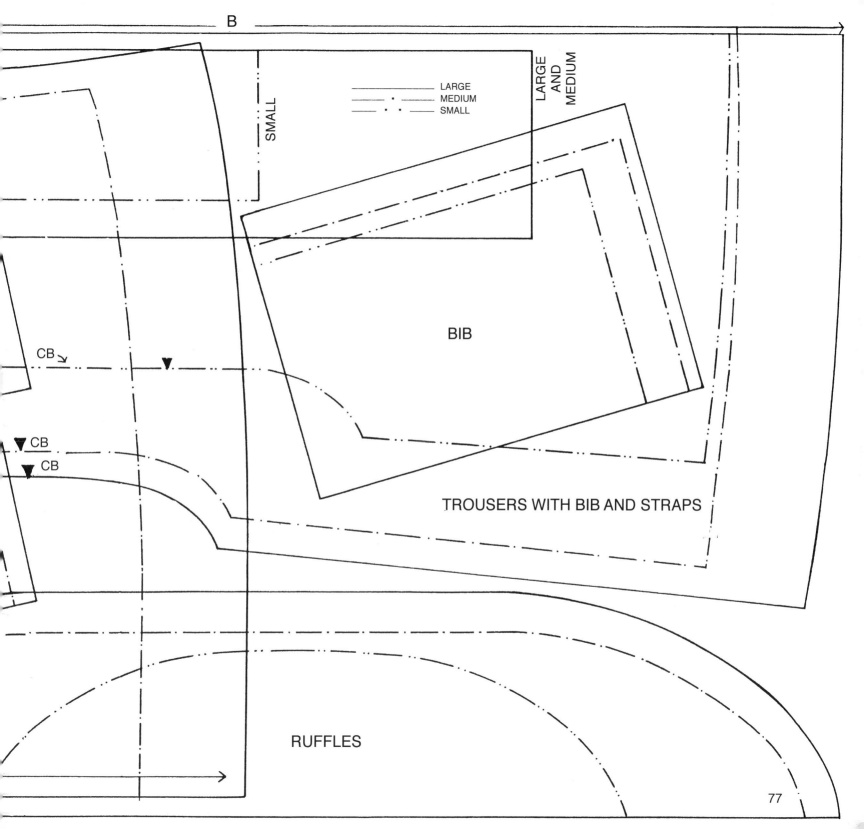

B

SMALL

LARGE AND MEDIUM

——————— LARGE
——·—·—— MEDIUM
——··—··— SMALL

BIB

CB

CB

CB

TROUSERS WITH BIB AND STRAPS

RUFFLES

77

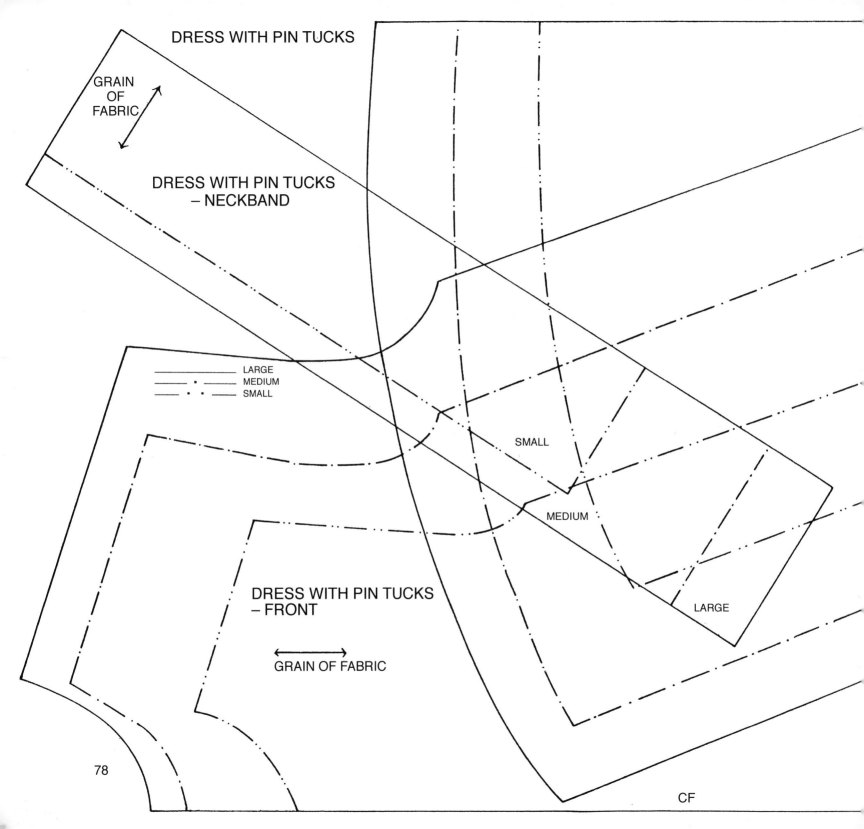

DRESS WITH PIN TUCKS

GRAIN
OF
FABRIC

DRESS WITH PIN TUCKS
– NECKBAND

LARGE
MEDIUM
SMALL

SMALL

MEDIUM

LARGE

DRESS WITH PIN TUCKS
– FRONT

GRAIN OF FABRIC

78

CF

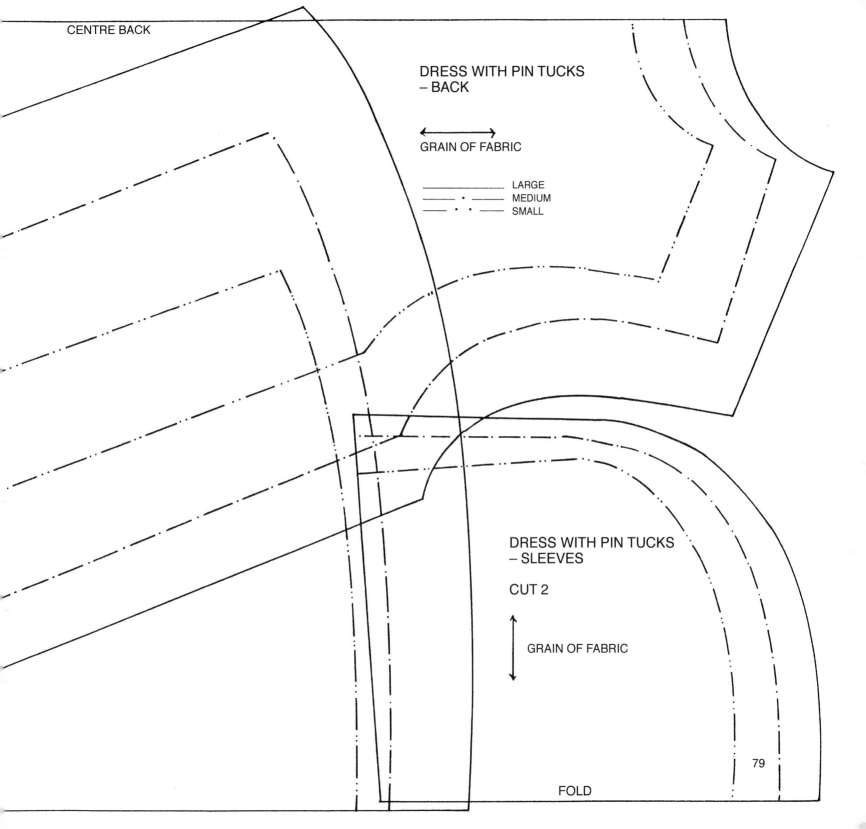

CENTRE BACK

DRESS WITH PIN TUCKS
– BACK

GRAIN OF FABRIC

	LARGE
	MEDIUM
	SMALL

DRESS WITH PIN TUCKS
– SLEEVES

CUT 2

GRAIN OF FABRIC

79

FOLD

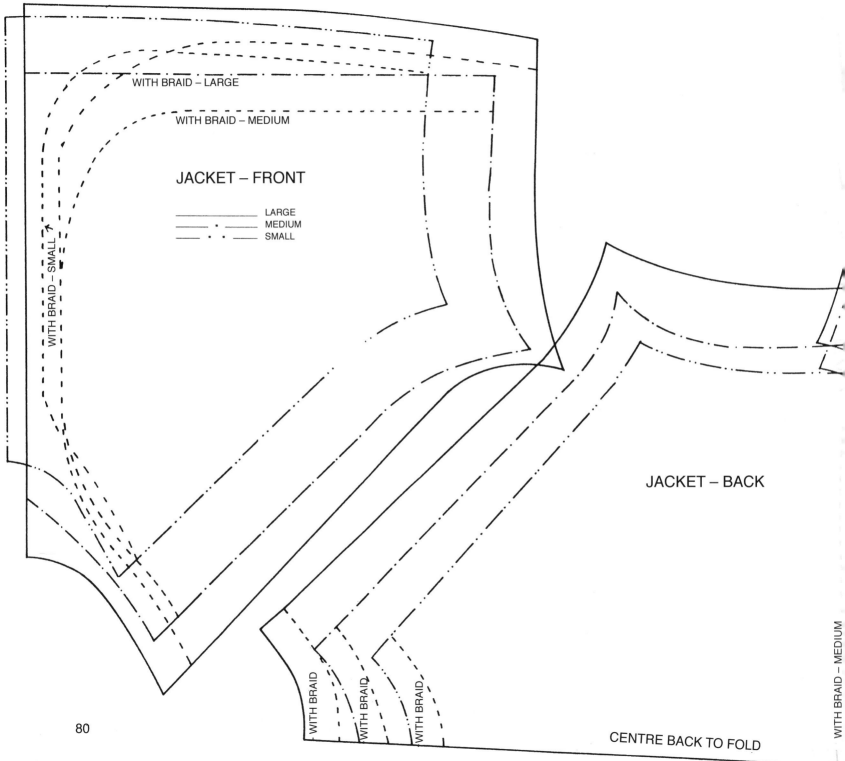

JACKET – BRAID-TRIMMED JACKET

WITH BRAID – LARGE

WITH BRAID – MEDIUM

JACKET – FRONT

LARGE
MEDIUM
SMALL

WITH BRAID – SMALL

JACKET – BACK

WITH BRAID

WITH BRAID

WITH BRAID

80

CENTRE BACK TO FOLD

WITH BRAID – MEDIUM

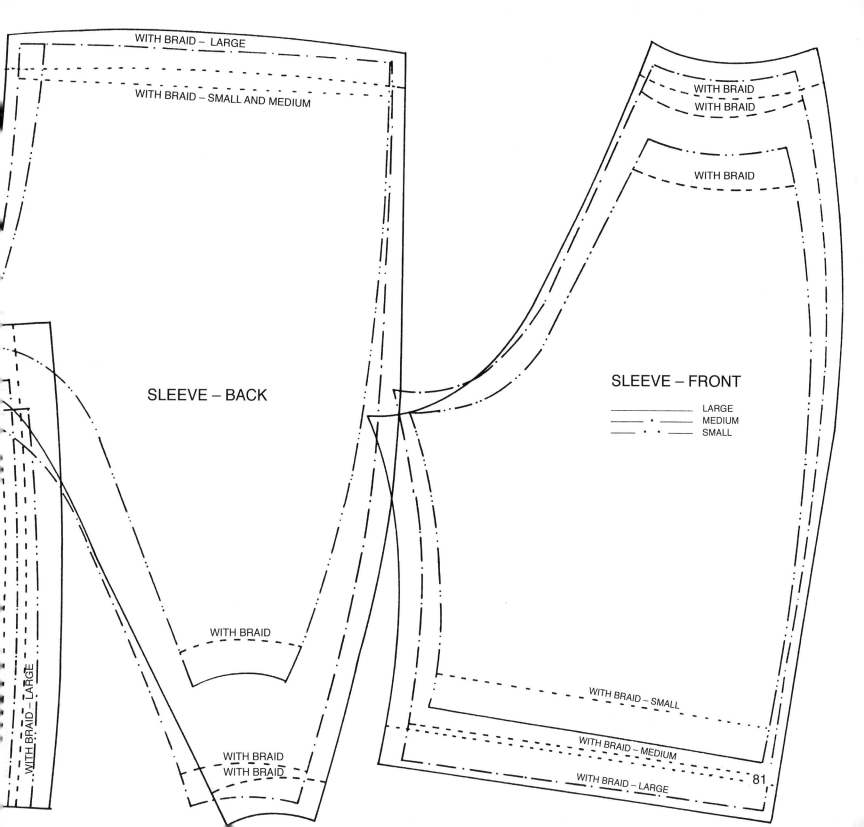

WITH BRAID – LARGE

WITH BRAID – SMALL AND MEDIUM

WITH BRAID

WITH BRAID

SLEEVE – BACK

SLEEVE – FRONT

LARGE
MEDIUM
SMALL

WITH BRAID – LARGE

WITH BRAID

WITH BRAID
WITH BRAID

WITH BRAID – SMALL

WITH BRAID – MEDIUM

WITH BRAID – LARGE

81

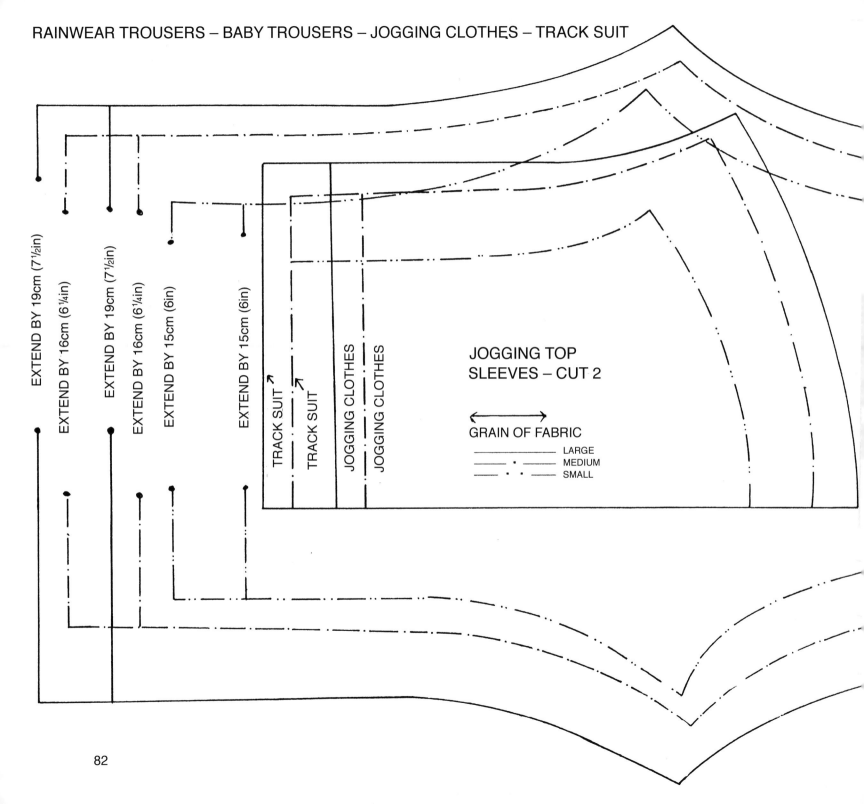

EXTEND BY 19cm (7½in)

EXTEND BY 16cm (6¼in)

EXTEND BY 19cm (7½in)

EXTEND BY 16cm (6¼in)

EXTEND BY 15cm (6in)

EXTEND BY 15cm (6in)

TRACK SUIT

TRACK SUIT

JOGGING CLOTHES

JOGGING CLOTHES

JOGGING TOP
SLEEVES – CUT 2

GRAIN OF FABRIC

LARGE
MEDIUM
SMALL

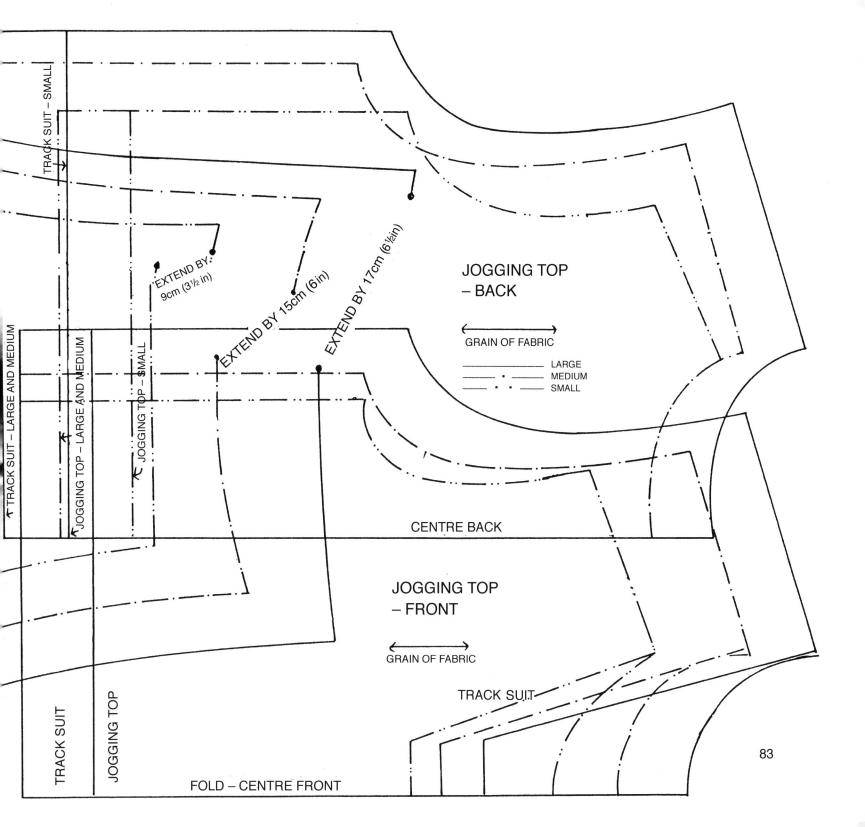

TRACK SUIT – SMALL

EXTEND BY:
9cm (3½ in)

EXTEND BY 15cm (6in)

EXTEND BY 17cm (6½in)

JOGGING TOP
– BACK

GRAIN OF FABRIC

LARGE
MEDIUM
SMALL

TRACK SUIT – LARGE AND MEDIUM

JOGGING TOP – LARGE AND MEDIUM

JOGGING TOP – SMALL

CENTRE BACK

JOGGING TOP
– FRONT

GRAIN OF FABRIC

TRACK SUIT

JOGGING TOP

TRACK SUIT

FOLD – CENTRE FRONT

83

ROMPER SUIT – SKI WEAR – PIERROT COSTUME

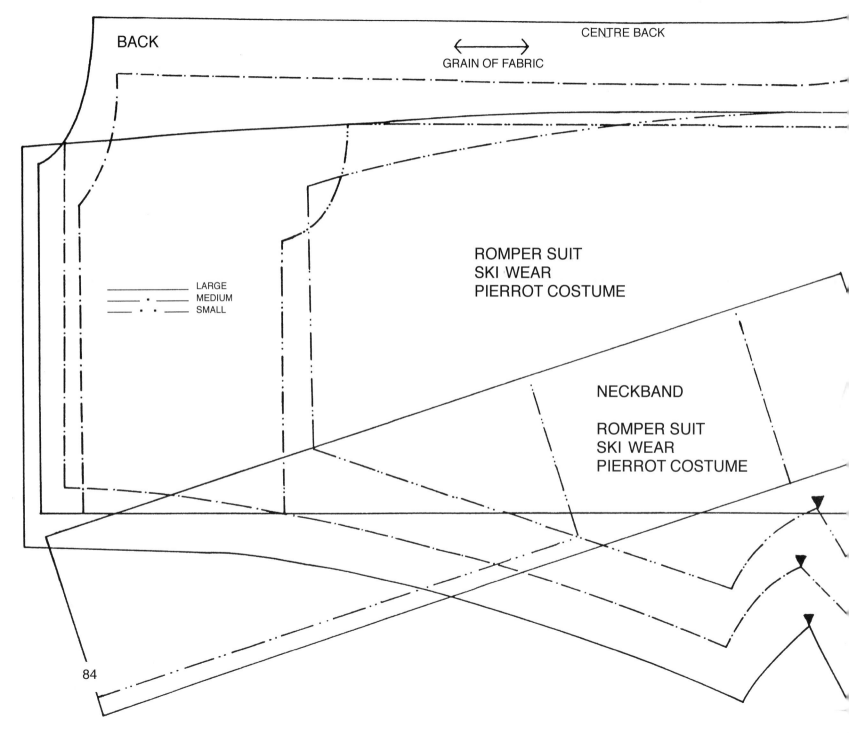

BACK

CENTRE BACK

GRAIN OF FABRIC

LARGE
MEDIUM
SMALL

ROMPER SUIT
SKI WEAR
PIERROT COSTUME

NECKBAND

ROMPER SUIT
SKI WEAR
PIERROT COSTUME

84

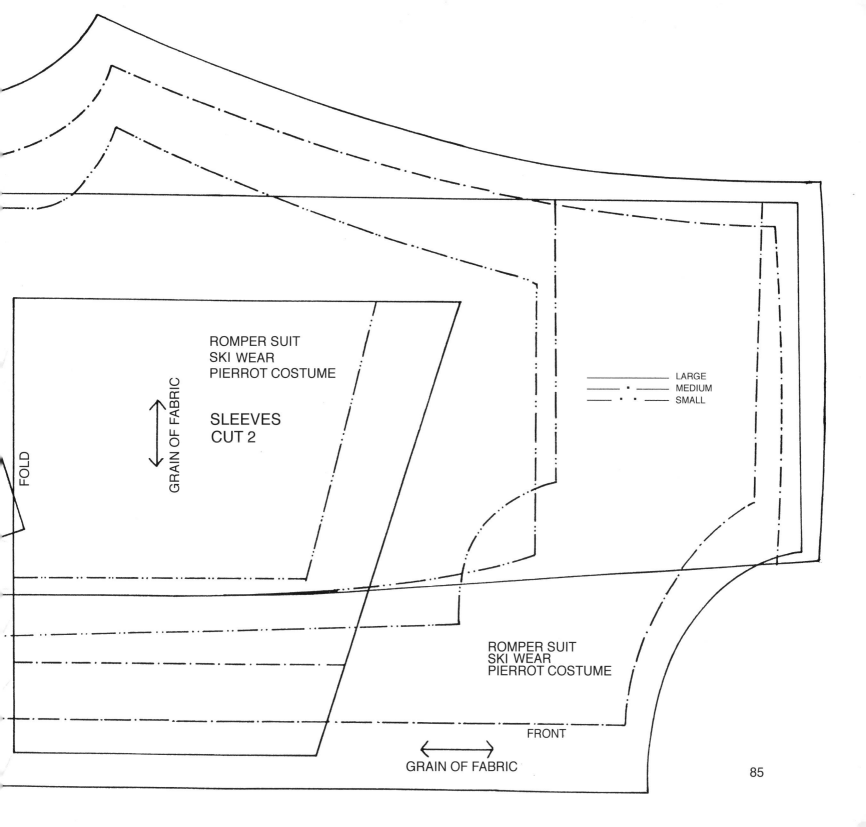

ROMPER SUIT
SKI WEAR
PIERROT COSTUME

GRAIN OF FABRIC

FOLD

SLEEVES
CUT 2

LARGE
MEDIUM
SMALL

ROMPER SUIT
SKI WEAR
PIERROT COSTUME

FRONT

GRAIN OF FABRIC

85

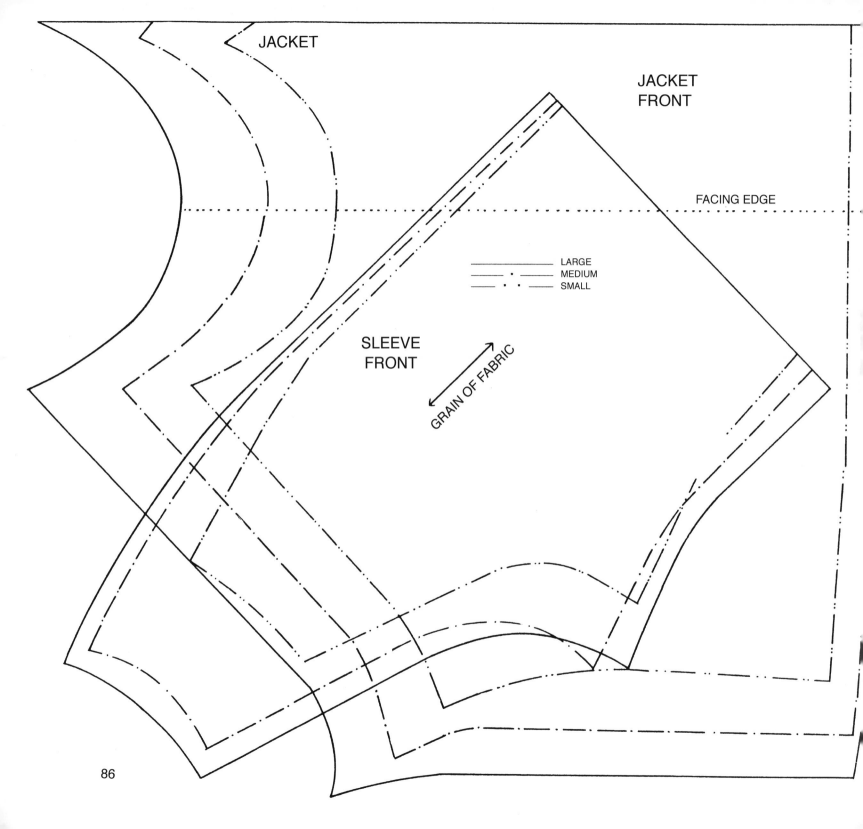

JACKET

JACKET
FRONT

FACING EDGE

LARGE
MEDIUM
SMALL

SLEEVE
FRONT

GRAIN OF FABRIC

86

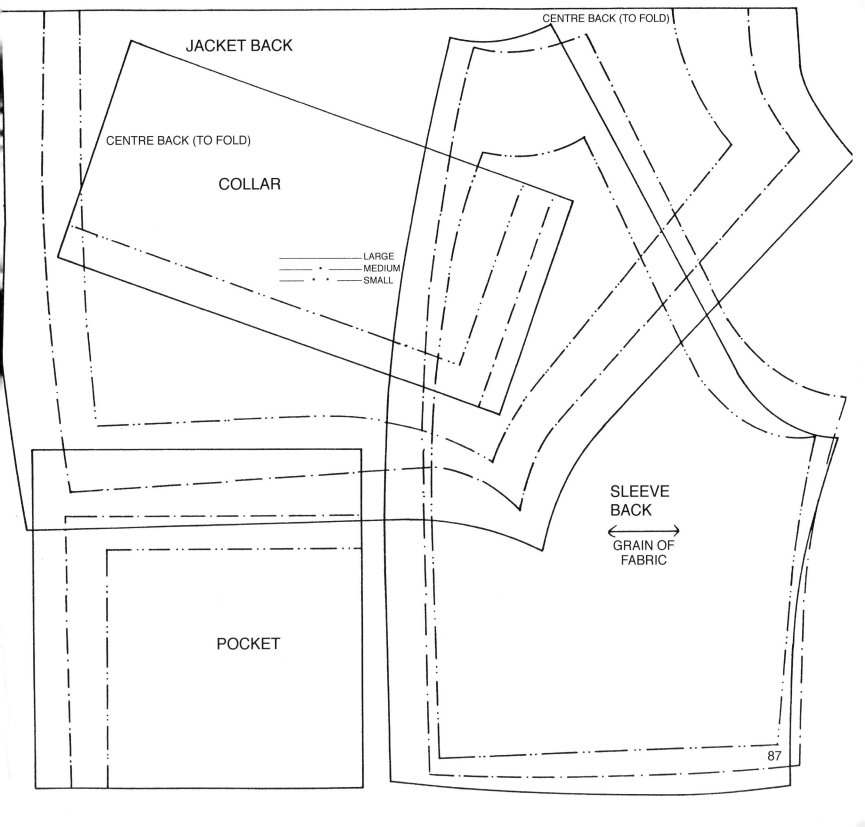

JACKET BACK

CENTRE BACK (TO FOLD)

CENTRE BACK (TO FOLD)

COLLAR

LARGE
MEDIUM
SMALL

SLEEVE
BACK

←——→
GRAIN OF
FABRIC

POCKET

87

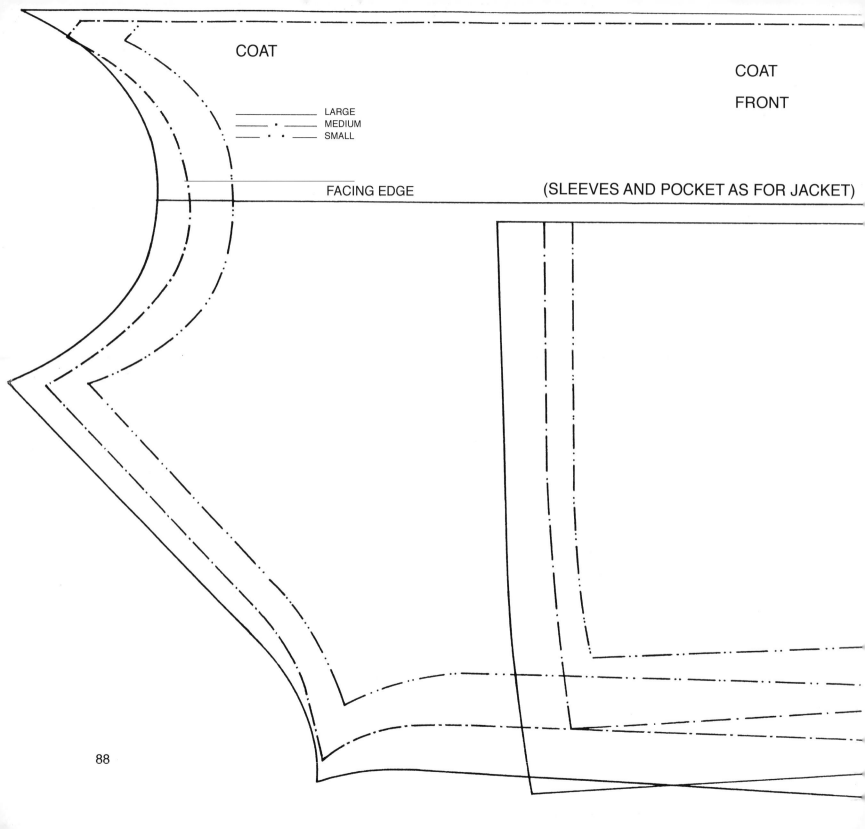

COAT

COAT

FRONT

LARGE
MEDIUM
SMALL

FACING EDGE

(SLEEVES AND POCKET AS FOR JACKET)

88

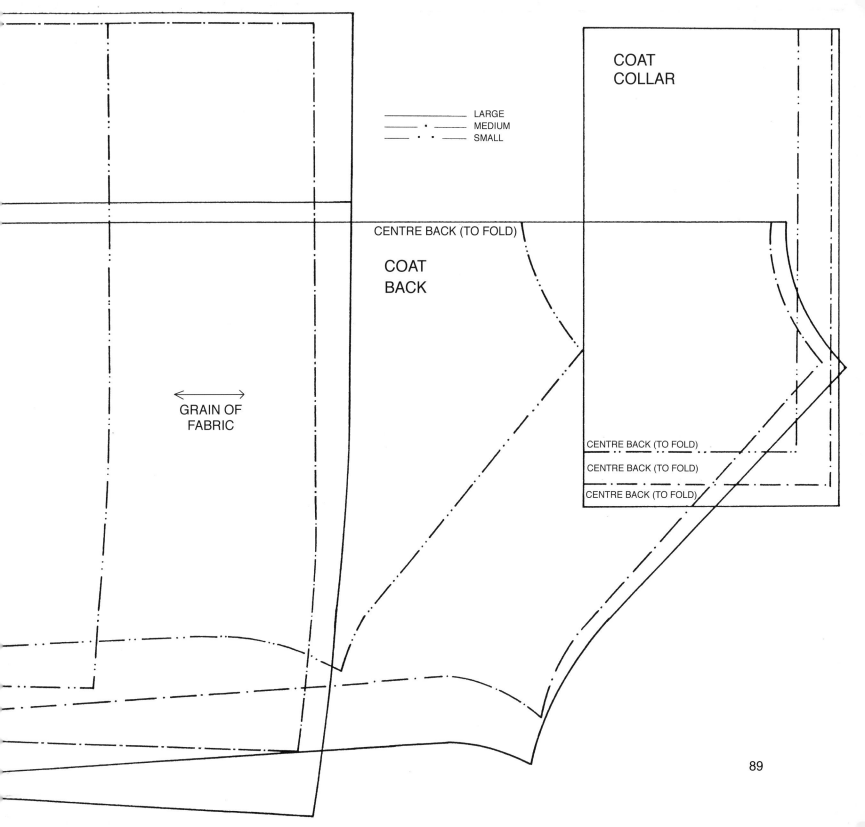

LARGE
MEDIUM
SMALL

COAT
COLLAR

CENTRE BACK (TO FOLD)

COAT
BACK

GRAIN OF
FABRIC

CENTRE BACK (TO FOLD)

CENTRE BACK (TO FOLD)

CENTRE BACK (TO FOLD)

89

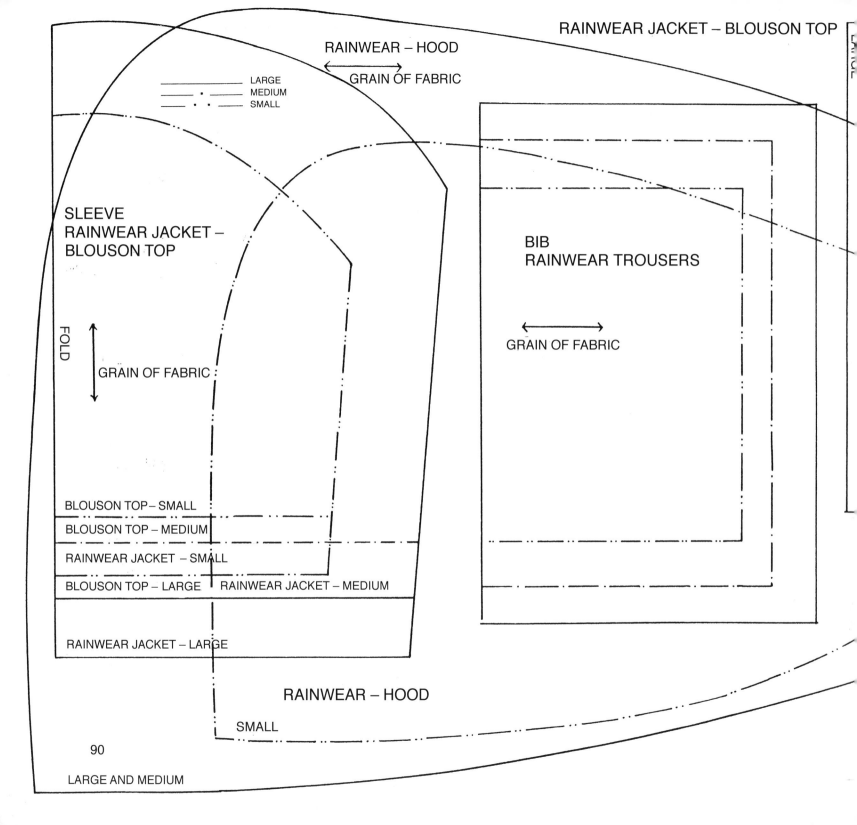

RAINWEAR JACKET – BLOUSON TOP

RAINWEAR – HOOD

GRAIN OF FABRIC

LARGE
MEDIUM
SMALL

SLEEVE
RAINWEAR JACKET –
BLOUSON TOP

FOLD

GRAIN OF FABRIC

BIB
RAINWEAR TROUSERS

GRAIN OF FABRIC

BLOUSON TOP – SMALL

BLOUSON TOP – MEDIUM

RAINWEAR JACKET – SMALL

BLOUSON TOP – LARGE   RAINWEAR JACKET – MEDIUM

RAINWEAR JACKET – LARGE

RAINWEAR – HOOD

SMALL

90

LARGE AND MEDIUM

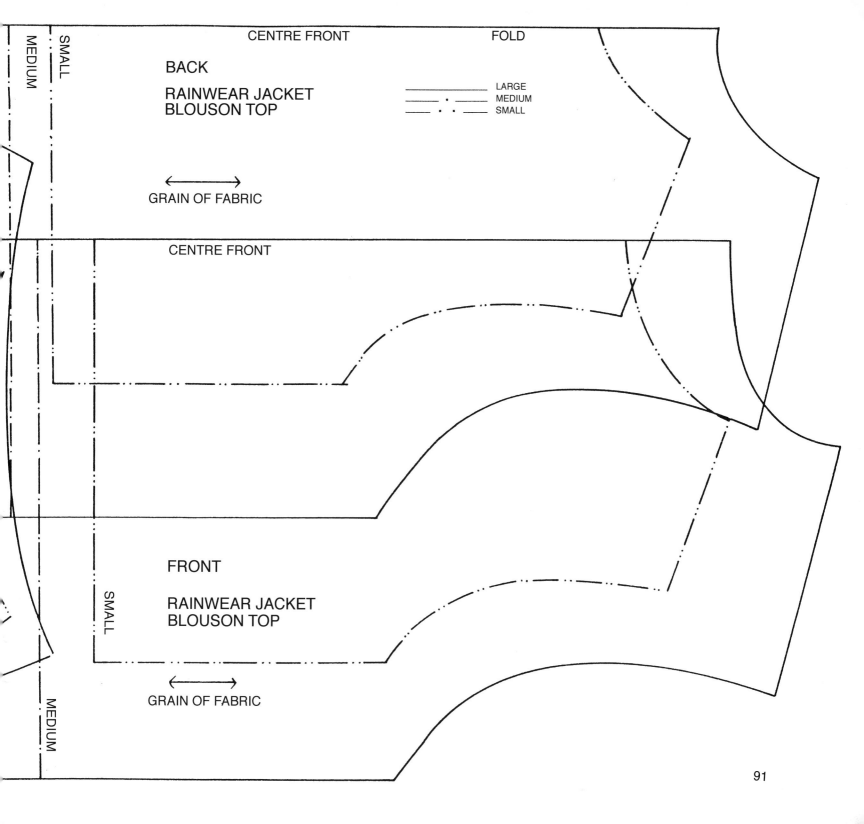

CENTRE FRONT   FOLD

BACK

RAINWEAR JACKET
BLOUSON TOP

————————— LARGE
———— · ———— MEDIUM
——— · · ——— SMALL

MEDIUM

SMALL

←——————→
GRAIN OF FABRIC

CENTRE FRONT

FRONT

RAINWEAR JACKET
BLOUSON TOP

SMALL

MEDIUM

←——————→
GRAIN OF FABRIC

91

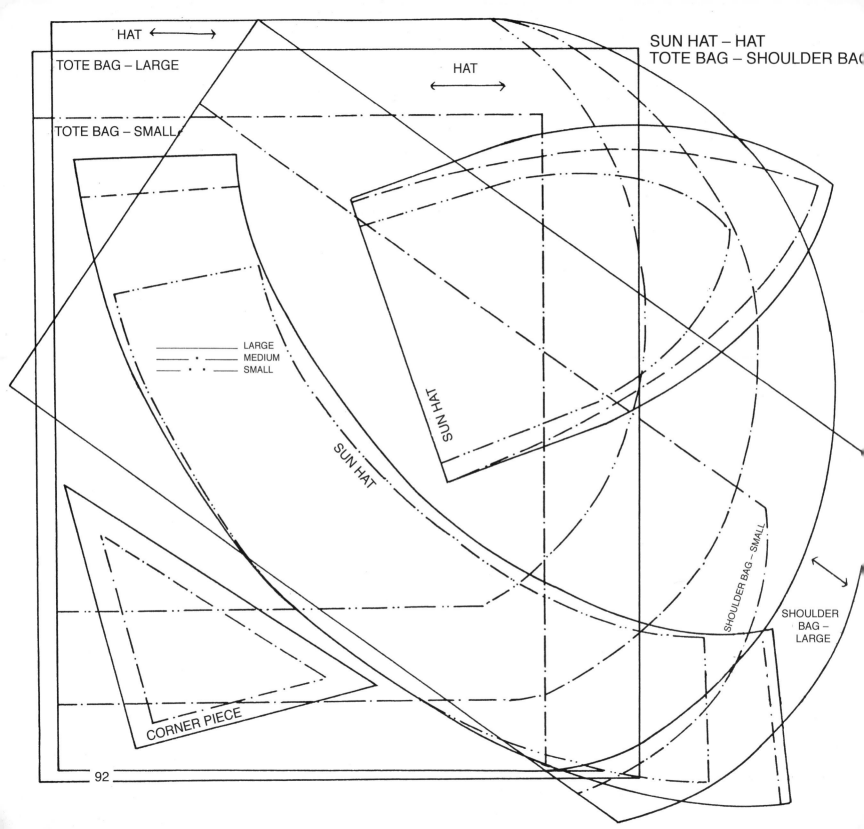

HAT ←——→

TOTE BAG – LARGE

TOTE BAG – SMALL

HAT ←——→

SUN HAT – HAT
TOTE BAG – SHOULDER BAG

LARGE
——·—— MEDIUM
——··—— SMALL

SUN HAT

SUN HAT

CORNER PIECE

SHOULDER BAG – SMALL

SHOULDER
BAG –
LARGE

92

Index

Baby skirt with straps 29
Baby trousers 20
Bias binding, attaching 57–8
Bikini top 30
Blouse with puffed sleeves 14, 16
Blouson jacket and skirt 41
Boxer shorts 25
Braid-trimmed jacket 36

Casing, stitching 58
Clown costume 50
Coat 45
Collar, lace 52
Culottes 17

Decoration ideas for bibs 60, 61
Dress with pin tucks 34
Dress with puffed sleeves 32, 33
Dressing gown 12
Dungarees 21

Gathering thread, stitching 59

Hat 53
Hat, sun 52

Jacket 44
Jogging clothes 37–8
Jogging top 37–8

Knickers 8
Knitted tops 50–52

Lace collar 52
Lace, attaching 56

Nightdress 10

Pajamas 37
Pantaloons 8
Patterned sweater 50–51
Petticoat 9
Pierrot costume 49–50
Pin tucks, stitching 59
Pleated trousers 18

Rainwear 48–9
Ribbed edges, attaching 57
Romper suit 42

Scarf 53
Short-sleeved T-shirt 14
Shorts 25
Shoulder bag 54
Ski wear 46
Skirt 26
Skirt with bib 28
Summer trousers 18
Sun hat 52
Swimming trunks 25

T-shirt 13
T-shirt, short-sleeved 14
Top 30
Tote bag 55
Track suit 40
Trousers, jogging 37
Trousers, pleated 18
Trousers with bib and straps 24

Underpants 7

Velcro strip, attaching 56
Vest 7

A CIP catalogue record for this book is available from
the British Library

ISBN 1 870586 32 8

Published by
David Porteous Editions
PO Box 5
Chudleigh
Newton Abbot
Devon TQ13 0YZ

Danish edition © 1988 Forlaget Kelmatis: Sy Dukketøj
English edition © 1997 David Porteous

Translated by Steven Harris
Printed in Hong Kong by Midas Printing Limited